Margaret Seeter

S0-BFR-374

Congressman
Jerry L. Pettis:
His Story

Congressman Jerry L. Pettis: His Story

by
Miriam Wood

Pacific Press Publishing Association
Mountain View, California
Oshawa, Ontario
Omaha, Nebraska

Dedication

To all young people who, because of the life of Jerry L. Pettis, will dare "to dream the impossible dream" this book is dedicated.

Copyright © 1977 by Pacific Press Publishing Association
Litho in United States
All rights reserved
Library of Congress Catalog No. 77-80683

Design by Eric Kreye

Foreword

It is, I think, appropriate that I state my purpose and objectives in writing this book. First, let me explain what I did *not* try to do—namely, I did not intend in any sense to write a definitive biography of Congressman Pettis in the various phases of his life. For example, I do not expect this book to be used as a research source concerning his attitude toward legislative issues which arose during his term of office. I will leave that field for political analysts. Neither did I attempt to document his keen business acumen which made him such a financially successful man, he who had started life with virtually nothing.

Therefore, what was left? The essence of the man himself—that is what I have tried to capture. His boundless energy, ambition, dedication to his many lives, and his search for ever higher and higher achievements. If I have succeeded in this goal, I am satisfied.

Miriam Wood

Acknowledgments

Any attempt to reconstruct the life of such a many-faceted person as Jerry L. Pettis is a formidable undertaking. Knowing this to be so, I enlisted the aid of scores of people who had been close to him through his lifetime or during certain phases of his life. I wish to express my eternal gratitude to these dear and loyal friends who took hours of their time to write their recollections or to be interviewed. Without their cooperation and encouragement this book could not have been written.

Miriam Wood

Prologue

Now the waiting and the hoping were over. The constant prayers which had been ascending from the hearts of the vigil-keepers— "Please, please, please, God—" were silenced. The unthinkable had happened. The unbelievable had come to pass. The unendurable must be endured, for it was now confirmed.

On the side of a lonely mountain in the San Gorgonio Pass, between Palm Springs and San Bernardino, California, lay the wreckage of a small private plane, clearly visible to eyes searching for it, yet hoping against hope never to see it. And in that wreckage—the end of a life. The end of the life of Congress Representative Jerry L. Pettis, who had served California's Thirty-seventh District so tirelessly, selflessly, and brilliantly for nine years. The date—February 14, 1975.

But even in the midst of the shattering event, too enormous to be comprehended, those who knew and loved him—and there were thousands—dimly sensed that his death was somehow the kind he would have wished. A man of the skies, with a spirit built to soar, to hover near the sun, like Icarus, it is impossible to imagine that he would ever have lived out an old age full of infirmities and limitations and diminishing powers.

Jerry Pettis was one of those rare human beings who are destined to leave behind them a legacy of "firsts." They see farther, attempt more, accomplish what others consider the impossible, are consumed with a vital fire. A log cabin or a poverty-stricken home in Arizona— the place and circumstances of their birth do not matter. They will fulfill their destiny. No matter what the odds, they will prevail. "Born of the sun, they travelled a short while towards the sun, and left the vivid air signed with their honour."

This is the story of such a man.

I Think Continually of Those Who Were Truly Great

I think continually of those who were truly great.
Who, from the womb, remembered the soul's history
Through corridors of light where the hours are suns
Endless and singing. Whose lovely ambition
Was that their lips, still touched with fire,
Should tell of the Spirit clothed from head to foot in song.
And who hoarded from the Spring branches
The desires falling across their bodies like blossoms.

What is precious is never to forget
The essential delight of the blood drawn from ageless springs
Breaking through rocks in worlds before our earth.
Never to deny its pleasure in the morning simple light
Nor its grave evening demand for love.
Never to allow gradually the traffic to smother
With noise and fog the flowering of the spirit.

Near the snow, near the sun, the highest fields
See how these names are fêted by the waving grass
And by the streamers of white cloud
And whispers of wind in the listening sky.
The names of those who in their lives fought for life
Who wore at their hearts the fire's centre.
Born of the sun they travelled a short while towards the sun
And left the vivid air signed with their honour.

—Stephen Spender.

Copyright 1934, renewed 1962, by Stephen Spender from *Selected Poems*.
Reprinted by permission of Random House, Inc.

Boy in a Hurry / 1

"Who knows? Maybe I'll be President someday!" declared Jerry Lyle Pettis at about the age of fourteen. From the perspective of today, this remark seems almost prophetic. In the context of the remark itself it elicited nothing but guffaws and loud derision from his audience. Of course the audience itself was hardly of the type to evaluate and appreciate what to them seemed the most ludicrous of statements. First of all, as he announced his probable future, he was engaged in the less-than-glamorous undertaking of milking a cow. Strapped to the cow's back was a most ingenious harness-type arrangement, an invention of Jerry's that held a book in position so that he could read and would not waste all those aggregate hours of milking.

The cows, though, simply went on munching their cuds, and his two friends, who had been scoffing at his lack of credibility, left the barn, chuckling. But Jerry went right on studying the dictionary, his favorite book. He was fascinated by words, always attempting to work newer and longer and more complicated ones into his vocabulary, sometimes with disastrous results.

The barn that echoed the "famous" remark was in Arizona, near Phoenix, where Jerry Lyle Pettis was born on July 18, 1916. The ranch didn't belong to his parents; he wasn't living with his family. Already, at fourteen, he had declared himself a man, taken on full responsibility for his own livelihood, found a friendly family who were staunch friends of his mother and father, and had bargained to live with them, doing all assigned chores, in order to finish his last two years at the Seventh-day Adventist secondary school in Phoenix.

Jerry's fierce need for independence may have been a cross for his family to bear, though time obscures the emotions and the heats of parent-child conflicts. When Jerry was born, his father was principal

9

of an integrated Mexican-American school, the first of its kind in the country; his mother was a teacher in the same school. Finally there were five Pettis children, four boys and one girl, with Jerry the oldest.

Perhaps Jerry's love of the "wide open spaces" came from his father, who soon found that the irksome routine of the teaching profession was too confining for his own independent spirit. Casting about for something more wild and free, he discovered that the office of state game warden was soon to be open. Just how he talked himself into the job, how he qualified for it, is not clear.

"Dad got a motorcycle and traveled over the state inspecting game sanctuaries," Jerry would later tell friends, in rare moments when he referred to his early life. "Once in a while he'd let me sit on the back of that old beat-up motorcycle, and we'd go flying down the Arizona roads."

One visualizes the small boy who, if he felt fear, would have refused flatly to admit it—the dusty Arizona "highways" (this was in the early 20s)—the long, long sweep of open country, the sagebrush, the cactus—in the spring, the desert carpeted with its own brand of beauty—the shimmering heat, the need to find a drink of cool water —lack of money for even a bottle of "pop"—and none of the discomfort making the slightest impression on the child clinging to his father's waist. Only the freedom, the speed, the feeling of "going someplace" mattered.

Alas for the vagaries of political life (and it is strange that Jerry himself developed no apprehension on this subject), for when a new state administration came into office, "their own" men came with it. Mr. Pettis found himself out of a job. A decision had to be made. Back home six mouths were open and hoping for food. Irksome though it be, he must return to his profession, teaching. But even that brand of employment wasn't easy to find—an Arizona job seemed unavailable. And so, with literally no money, but with much determination, he decided to move his family to the greener pastures of California— greener both literally and figuratively. Jerry went along. He was only twelve, but he left part of his heart in Arizona, where it remained for the rest of his life.

As a matter of fact, he followed his heart back there in just two years. He had taken his first two years of secondary school in Sebastopol and then at Healdsburg, both very small towns in northern California. Unfortunately, parochial school teachers' salaries were hardly adequate. The Pettis family had to content themselves with a roof over their heads and barely enough food to sustain themselves.

Probably these early years of deprivation and humiliation left their mark on Jerry, for as the years came and went and his life developed, he feared finally only one thing—poverty. He feared it not only for himself, but for everyone. To him, as an adult, and later a United States Congressman, it appeared almost obscene that human beings created in the image of God should have to worry about the barest essentials of living.

At fourteen, though, he could not be expected to pursue such far-reaching and philosophical thoughts. And even so, it is doubtful that he would have expressed them to his family, who had not an easy role themselves to play, much like chickens who have inadvertently hatched a swan. Jerry was always a private person; he, who appeared on the surface to be so open and gregarious, possessed deep inner recesses and citadels that probably were penetrated by only one other human being in his lifetime—his wife Shirley. But that would come many years later.

"I'm going back to Arizona and live with the Mundalls," he coolly and calmly announced to his parents, with no previous warning.

"You're going to do *what*?" his father roared.

Intimidated not at all, Jerry repeated his declaration of independence.

"And how do you know they'll take you?" was his mother's apprehensive question.

"Because I just know," he stated characteristically, certain that no plan he made for himself could go awry.

Momentarily struck dumb, his father rallied. "How do you expect to get there? I don't have one dime to send you on a bus, and I wouldn't send you if I could. You belong here with your own family."

"I'll hitchhike," was Jerry's clincher. No amount of persuasion could change his mind. He was the product of two strong and determined parents. It is possible that they thought he would "learn his lesson." And it is equally possible that they felt, as so many other parents have felt throughout the ages, unable to cope with an unusually strong-willed, ambitious offspring. For Jerry had already determined that he would graduate from college. When one remembers that the country was in the grip of the Great Depression of the 1930s, that there was absolutely no money to spare in the family, if his ambitions seemed unrealistic to his parents and brothers and sister, one could hardly blame them for their doubts.

And so Jerry *did* hitchhike to Arizona. And he did appear on the doorstep of the Mundall family. And they did take him in. And he was able to work for them and somehow manage to earn his tuition and graduate from the Arizona Academy in Phoenix two years later, when he was sixteen. Not only did he read the dictionary strapped to the harness on the cow's back, he did much of his studying in the same way. He seemed able to get along with almost no sleep; later on, during his college years, it was not at all unusual for him to work nearly all night in the barns, go to class all day, study, and go back to work, with perhaps half an hour of deep sleep snatched somewhere during the day.

Between fourteen and sixteen, Jerry developed an interest which remained throughout his life and influenced his action—flying. The kindly Mundall family, who regarded him as one of their own, made it a point to take the whole family to the Arizona State Fair every year, held in Phoenix. (After all, nearly everything was free to be looked at—the animal exhibits, canned goods, quilts, etc. Where better to take a brood of teen-agers?)

Aviation was certainly in—if not its infancy—its very early adolescence at that time. However, an enterprising flier owned a small plane which he had brought to the fair, offering rides for a small price. (No one seems able to remember the exact amount of cash involved.) Of course this proved to be the star attraction of the fair. All the teen-agers and most of the adults stood about, the more courageous calculating just how they could spare the price of a ride and the more affluent climbing into the plane for the short spin over the city, emerging, in some cases, pale and shaken, but resembling gods in the eyes of their earth-bound compatriots.

"I am going up in the plane!" Jerry burst out.

"Using what for money?" his friends scoffed.

"I'll figure out a way. Just you wait and see," Jerry grimly promised.

How he accomplished the impossible—the raising of the money —is shrouded in the mists of unclear memory. Probably he found a kind friend and used all his persuasive powers. But how he got the money isn't important. What's important is that he got it—and he *flew*.

Seldom has the world seen a more significant meeting of man and machine. In later life he would say that nothing, nothing could ever match the exhilaration of those first moments in the air, the feeling of soaring, free and light and gloriously above it all, the feeling of oneness with the universe.

"I'M GOING TO BE A PILOT SOMEDAY!" were his first words upon landing.

Lester and Raymond didn't take him seriously. And you can't really blame them. But Jerry did become not only a pilot, but a pioneer in many phases of aviation; and he carried with him until the day he died a commercial pilot's license entitling him to fly any kind of plane.

Jerry's determination never to be bested at anything sometimes translated itself into scuffles, both verbal and physical, with his foster brothers, Lester and Raymond. For instance, there was the episode of the picnic and the horse.

"Let's go to Squaw Peak for a picnic!" one of the teen-agers suggested. Mrs. Mundall agreed to the plan. (Her warmhearted, loving supervision of her "flock" doubtless had a profound effect upon Jerry's sense of security.)

"How'll we get there?" was the next question. Squaw Peak was several miles from the ranch.

After a moment's thought, Mr. Mundall announced, "I have it figured out. We'll just clean out the wagon, hitch up the two horses to it, and away we'll go."

But this didn't suit the boys.

"Poking along in the wagon's no fun!" they declared vehemently. "Let's just hitch one horse to the wagon, and then we can take turns riding the other horse. That way we can gallop back and forth and really have a great time."

Seeing no particular objection to the plan, though it obviously lacked logic, the wiser, older man agreed, totally unaware that he was an unwitting accomplice to a "situation" which would develop.

Of course it was much more fun to ride the horse than to creak along in the wagon, but the boys dutifully worked out a time system, whereby each one spent a certain amount of time on horseback, went off on side-trip explorations if he so desired, and then reported back to the wagon so that the next boy could have his riding turn. All went well on the way to Squaw Peak, or seemed to, but the impatience which was another major factor in Jerry's nature began to build up to quite a head of steam. He contained his energy during the picnic. But why in the world, once the picnic lunch was eaten, and it was time to leave, should he spend his precious time ambling along in the old creaky wagon? He had things to do. As for the other boys—well, they could fend for themselves. (Later in life he totally overcame that kind of self-absorption. But one cannot help admiring, almost against his will, the daring and audacity of the "stranger in their midst" who was about to "kidnap" one of the family horses.)

For that's exactly what he did. He was to ride horseback first. Jumping astride the creature, he took off like the wind. The rest of the family followed at their enforced, sedate pace.

Lester began looking at his watch.

"Jerry should be back by now," he fumed. "It's time for my turn."

"Oh, he'll show up any minute, I'm sure," Mrs. Mundall soothed, used to the pullings and tuggings of the strong young wills.

But he didn't show up. And pretty soon it became obvious that he wasn't *going* to show up!

"Why, he's going to ride that horse right on home!" Lester exclaimed unbelievingly. He thought a moment, his face set in lines as determined as Jerry's.

"Whoa!" he called to the patient creature pulling the wagon. Leaping out, before anyone realized what he was doing, he began to unhitch the horse from the wagon.

"What in the world—" the bewildered passengers began.

"This is one time he's gone too far. I won't take it. Just wait here, and I'll be back for you," Lester called to them over his shoulder, as he took off, bareback on the surprised horse, digging his heels into its sides. Suddenly getting into the spirit of the situation, the puzzled horse outdid itself. Before long, Lester had an unsuspecting Jerry in sight. (The latter hadn't been able to resist taking a small detour to investigate something which had caught his interest.)

For a few moments the two boys raced side by side through the desert, the horses' sides touching, each boy determined not to give an

14

inch, though it became increasingly clear that for once the patient Lester had had every ounce of provocation he was prepared to take. Visionary though he was, Jerry was also a realist. He knew when to "cut his losses." Bowing to the inevitable, he brought the horse to a standstill, and jumped off—but not without one last gesture of undefeatedness. While Lester was skidding to a halt beyond him, and dismounting, quick as lightning, Jerry took off the bridle of "his" horse, slapped it smartly on its rump and told it to go home. In other words, if Jerry Lyle Pettis was to suffer the ignominy of being dismounted in the middle of the desert, no one else would ride the horse home either.

"Why, you—" Lester shouted, characterizing his erstwhile friend with a string of highly descriptive adjectives, none of them flattering.

Of course the inevitable happened. When two young males find themselves locked in verbal combat, the situation usually disintegrates rapidly into physical combat. This situation was no exception. Both Jerry and Lester later characterized subsequent events as "a good scuffle"—and they had the bruises to prove it.

Finally the two gladiators rode back, double, on the patient beast who had witnessed their fight in the wilds of the Arizona desert. Little was said as they hitched the horse to the wagon and began the plodding trip home. Fortunately, the horse Jerry had dismissed so unceremoniously had found its way back to the ranch, or he would have had to go in search of it—which would have been poetic justice.

Finally it was graduation time. In the 30s, graduation pictures were "big," and students eagerly awaited the outcome of the photographer's genius.

For once, the odds caught up with the sixteen-year-old who recognized no limitations. Simply stated, he had no money for pictures. He prayed about it. He mulled over idea after idea; he explored every possibility. Stalemate. His foster brother Raymond posed excitedly for his pictures and now awaited his proofs.

Jerry, proud and seemingly unconcerned, said nothing of his heartache. It was impossible for him to admit it hurt. He simply grew another coating of protective "shell" around his heart.

But dear Mrs. Mundall! She knew. She called him aside, very quietly.

"Jerry," she told him, "you'll only graduate from the academy once. I want you to have your pictures. I've saved back some of my egg money, and I'm going to pay for them."

He couldn't believe it, as he gazed into those kind and loving eyes. After all, behind the bravado and the undefeatedness and the hard-workingness was a boy scarcely out of childhood.

"Thank you," he choked.

And then his spirits soared. Never did an academy senior so enjoy getting his pictures taken, and never did he so enjoy autographing them for his friends. Every picture had a destination, particularly for the feminine contingent of the class. He had a "way with the ladies" —very innocent, in those days, and exemplary all the days of his life. But girl friends he had, and would-be girl friends. Someone took occasion to chide him for his "eye for pretty girls." He didn't deny the charge. Calmly he announced, "When I marry, I plan to come home from work every day to a *pretty* wife."

Jerry graduated. His next move was already charted in his mind. No uncertainty. He would go immediately to Pacific Union College, a Seventh-day Adventist college, near Napa, California, and he would enroll. It would never have occurred to him to attend anything but this kind of school, for he was now a baptized church member, and a committed one, which he remained throughout his lifetime.

Of course he had heard that you had to have "so much" for a deposit in order even to enroll at P.U.C., and you had to—But he would manage somehow. Hadn't he always?

Mildred Mundall Falcomer sums up those years from fourteen to sixteen when Jerry was a member of the family:

"Jerry was always quick and eager for learning. He had no time to waste. He was perhaps more aggressive than most of his friends. These are all good traits. The young people knew real poverty in those days, and if you didn't really set goals and strive hard, and resign yourself to doing without many of the niceties and even necessities, you never got anywhere. We were all immensely proud of Jerry's accomplishments. Who knows? Perhaps he *would* have been President someday, but apparently it wasn't in God's plan for him."

In the early summer of 1933, Jerry Lyle Pettis was ready for P.U.C. Was P.U.C. ready for Jerry Lyle Pettis?

Jerry on Campus /2

When P.U.C. President W. E. Nelson was told that a good-looking, attractive, mannerly, determined young man was insisting on an interview with him, he was puzzled.

"I don't quite understand. Has he come here to college to enroll? If so, he doesn't need to see me. You know how to instruct him in the regular procedures and routine," he told his secretary a bit reproachfully.

She gulped. "Of course I know all that, President Nelson. But—well—this is a very *unusual* case, and I think you'd better see him!"

Taken aback by the insistence of his usually docile secretary, President Nelson bowed to the inevitable. More than that, though, his curiosity was aroused. Students were his business; he knew all varieties. What could be so different about this one?

Actually, when the tall, slender, brown-haired young man was ushered in, he didn't seem to be all that different. Well, certainly he was more self-possessed than the average sixteen-turning-seventeen. He didn't cower in terror before the somewhat majestic mien of President Nelson, a man who generated an atmosphere of reverence and hushed voices among the student body. He looked the president right in the eyes and, after exchanging the usual amenities, announced, "I'm here to enroll in college. I'll need to work all I can this summer to get a credit built up, and so I'd like to start immediately."

Still mystified, President Nelson murmured, "Well, I suppose it might be possible to find something for you to do. Of course you understand that you have to have a certain percentage in cash as a down payment?"

There was a moment of silence. Then Jerry answered quietly, "Well, you see, I don't have *any* cash. As a matter of fact, I hitchhiked up here."

President Nelson didn't know whether to be exasperated or sympathetic. It was the depth of the depression, and many Seventh-day Adventist young people were wanting a college education; he had heard the story so many times before; if he could only wave a financial wand, he would take them all in and educate them free, but he *did* have a board and a business manager, and—and yet—.

Somehow the sheer audacity and courage of this rawboned, deeply tanned boy on the other side of the desk got through his own common sense, which told him, logically, that it couldn't be done. President Nelson began to hedge a bit. And Jerry began to hope, though if the truth were known, he had never for a moment doubted that "something" would work out.

Trying to be gruff, and not succeeding very well (did the boy look as though he could use a good meal?) President Nelson demanded,— "What kind of work can you do?"

Now they were getting somewhere.

"I can do anything and everything that needs doing on a farm," Jerry promptly replied. "I worked the last two years on a dairy farm in Arizona."

"You mean you can milk cows?" the president asked in astonishment.

"All day and all night if I have to," Jerry calmly announced.

Fate, that indefinable element in the lives of human beings, had played its part for Jerry, as it was so often to do in his subsequent life. Only the day before, Mr. Baldwin, the college farm manager, had talked with President Nelson over a most serious problem.

"How in the world am I going to run this big college farm and dairy?" he had asked. "All the students we get nowadays seem to be city boys. They don't know whether tomatoes grow above or under the ground. And they have no idea as to what end of a cow should be milked. After all, the farm is supposed to provide much of the food for the college—you know we can't afford to buy everything at market prices—and it also should provide work for students—but I'm really stumped."

(Parenthetically, it might be noted that the philosophy of Seventh-day Adventist education has always been to provide some physical work for students, both because this is a healthful thing to do and in those days it enabled students to attend who otherwise would never have been able to do so. In recent years, the custom of using student labor on college farms and in industries has not been so prevalent as it was then. This trend is to be deplored, since many educators, both religious and secular, have now embraced the idea of student labor as one of the finest ever originated.)

Picking up the phone, President Nelson called the farm manager's office.

"Mr. Baldwin," he said, in his distinctive, very high voice, "I have a young man in my office whom I think you might like to meet. He wants to work his way through college on the farm. He's just spent two years on a dairy farm in Arizona."

The delighted explosions of sound on the other end of the line were obvious. Jerry didn't need President Nelson's broad smile to tell him that it was going to work out. "Thank You, dear heavenly Father," he breathed silently. Actually, he'd done a lot of praying on that long walk up the winding road to P.U.C., the "College in the Crater," the crater now extinct, fortunately.

Though Mr. Baldwin didn't go out on a limb by promising Jerry full employment for the duration of his stay on "the hill," as P.U.C. was affectionately known, he put him to work immediately. Within a week he phoned President Nelson.

"Jerry Pettis is here to stay," he announced firmly.

And so, for the next five years, Jerry would get up at three o'clock every morning and milk cows before reporting to class. (Taking college in five years instead of four was his only concession to the realities of life.) His starting salary was 18 cents an hour, but by working the year around tirelessly, he managed to save enough money to pay his own tuition and help his sister one year when she badly wanted to attend college.

Jerry's financial inventiveness asserted itself in the most unique ways. During the summer one of his assignments was to help process for canning the vegetables grown on the farm. (It would be years before freezing was popularized.) He was given for his own use the undersized carrots, turnips, tomatoes, and other produce. Somehow he got acquainted with a friend who worked in a shredded-wheat plant not too far away and arranged to buy large bags of broken shredded-wheat biscuits for a dollar. And since Mr. Baldwin allowed the "dairy boys" all the milk they could drink, Jerry boasted that there were times when his monthly food bill was as low as seven dollars.

One visualizes, though, with a certain lump in the throat, the intrepid boy, sitting in his sparsely furnished room (his foster mother had given him whatever castoffs she could spare) eating his lonely way through his discarded vegetables, broken shredded wheat, and milk, day after day.

But Jerry had absolutely no capacity or time for self-pity. A life was out there waiting to be lived. He plunged into campus activities.

Entering his life at this point was a man who would bring to bear a greater influence than any other—the late Dr. Charles E. Weniger, professor of speech. In him, Jerry apparently found the ideal that somehow he needed, in spite of his exterior independence. And Dr. Weniger found in Jerry the son he never had, the brilliant, malleable youth waiting to be shaped into "A Man for All Seasons." Jerry worked for Dr. Weniger as his assistant during the college years—in addition, of course, to his night dairy work, for the latter alone would not have paid his expenses.

It is important here to characterize Charles Weniger, for in his own way he too was a unique human being. First of all, he was a peerless teacher. He made teaching not a profession but an art, an exercise in breathless anticipation for his students. Impossible? Well, not for him. Next, he was one of the most faultlessly groomed men one would ever meet. His manners were so impeccable, his attitude so gracious, his demeanor so faultless, that it is impossible to measure his impact on the wide-eyed, awkward, all-elbows-and-knees young students who saw, for the first time, the full dimensions of development of which a human being is capable, socially. And his religious dedication was just as strong, just as positive. All his students learned as much from being in his presence as they learned from his classes; and considering that his classes were sheer perfection, what more can be said?

It was not, though, a sentimental attachment; Dr. Weniger had no intention of letting Jerry get by with anything; he did not pamper any of his students, and perhaps he was even harder than usual on Jerry. The latter conceived the idea of organizing a new club—a speech club named The Forum—and, somewhat to his embarrassment, he was immediately elected president of the club. As the years progressed, he became used to "the presidency," since he was always president of one organization or another. On a present-day campus, with its freedoms and activities, a speech club would certainly seem the mildest of activities, but in the small, isolated religious college, some of The Forum's activities marked great innovations—particularly that of a kind of freedom of speech. (Even a student such as Jerry was not out of step with the culture in which he lived; he conformed to the rules, first because he was conscientious, and second because he was just plain sensible. In those days you lined up, or you lined out.)

However, the restrictiveness of the atmosphere did not keep his thoughts from racing into the future. For instance, he used to argue passionately for an amendment that would enable a 21-year-old to become President of the United States. One of his close friends, Charles Anderson (now for many years a psychiatrist) was no unworthy antagonist in an argument. He always took the position that such a President wouldn't have any experience behind him to make it possible for him to function effectively.

"But think of the energy he'd have!" was Jerry's triumphant rejoinder. They argued and debated this issue during Forum meetings.

During another session of the "famous" club (usually held fairly early on Saturday night, before the main entertainment of the evening) Dr. Weniger suggested that members prepare political nominations—any member could nominate any other member for any political office, as long as the time held out.

"I nominate Jerry Lyle Pettis for Governor of California," declared the same Charles Anderson, and proceeded to explain why Pettis would be needed to take over the supposed shambles that would be the state "after" Upton Sinclair. As it turned out, Frank Merriam defeated Sinclair for Governor in 1934, so Jerry's political expertise was not called upon at that point.

Jerry also knew how to whip up an argument, and then sit back with a calm, bemused smile, as group members rushed at one another in a metaphorical tangle of rhetoric. One sentiment for which he was famous—and which he believed not one whit—was his historic "I am an advocate of Platonic love" declaration. Whatever else, it certainly was an attention-getter. Dozens of his friends felt it their mission to change his mind, though if they had thought it through, they could not have escaped knowing that Jerry was just being—

Jerry. He was as attractive to the girls as ever, and they to him, though how he managed to carry on so many active romances, with his schedule, will forever remain a mystery.

And he was still in love—Platonically or otherwise—with big words. On a lecture circuit which included Pacific Union College, the distinguished political scientist, Dr. Alonzo Baker, used the word "catastrophically." Jerry was instantly enamored with that word and went about the campus using it for days. (Fate, as we have pointed out previously, played a major role in the life of Jerry Pettis. Later on, Dr. Baker was to become one of his chief political advisers, and one of those who helped him make his first decision to run for Congress.) Then, however, Jerry was still developing. Other favorite big words were "cacophony" and "miscellany." Then he discovered "omnivorous." There was one small difficulty there, however. He put the accent on the third syllable rather than the second. Of course, someone took glee in pointing out his error.

Also there was the unfortunate incident of his declaring publicly that the students were indulging in "foolish gestation." Horrified, Charles took him aside to explain the gravity of what he had said. (In a small Seventh-day Adventist college in 1933–34, such a blunder *was* serious!)

Wide-eyed, Jerry listened. "Why, I thought it was just a variation on 'jesting,' " he defended himself.

These small embarrassments and minor setbacks did not whittle away at his self-confidence. If he bled, it was inwardly. If he suffered, it was silently. On the outside, things always remained the same. His time for study was limited, though his grades were good, and would have been excellent had he not worked around the clock, plus participating in every phase of campus life. Even yet, Milton Lee, who has spent a lifetime as a Christian missionary in the Orient, has not forgotten the time in an advanced speech class when Jerry simply had no time to prepare a speech, though it was one of Dr. Weniger's cardinal rules that unpreparedness was unthinkable, and, of course, unacceptable.

When Milton was called on, confidently he rose to his feet. A quiet, controlled, dignified young man, he delivered his carefully prepared, well-reasoned speech, and then sat down, quite satisfied with his performance. Next, Jerry Pettis. The latter, without the flicker of an eyelash, swung smoothly into his topic—history does not record what it was—presented his facts, marshalled his conclusion, and sat down, as unruffled as he always was. Milton, however, can be pardoned for a moment of self-righteousness. After all, *he* had prepared. Jerry had not. The outcome in grades was bound to tell the story.

The story? Jerry Pettis: A. Milton Lee: B.

Of course, money—or the lack of it—was an ever-present problem. Jerry was constantly on the alert for new ways to solve the dilemma. For instance, during the summer of 1935, there appeared the Camay soap contest. This was the day of contests in which ''in 25 words or less'' entrants declared why a particular soap or some other product was superior to any other. The prizes, in terms of today's TV game shows, seem pitifully small, but they were magnificent beyond belief to the dazzled eyes of ''depression children.'' In this case, the prize was a new Pontiac convertible and 1000 gallons of gasoline. Jerry spent much time and thought with his slogan and came up with this entry: ''Companion of Beauty and Loveliness.'' It simply never occurred to him that he wouldn't win. He had it all planned—he would sell the car and would travel via ''Easy Street'' for the remainder of his college education. Alas, when the winner was announced, it was *not* J. L. Pettis. Loyal friends assured him that his slogan was better—there was something the matter with the judges. After an hour or so of gloom, he dismissed the whole incident and went on to the next item on his agenda.

His cheerful ''Good morning'' as he entered the men's residence dormitory (Grainger Hall) each morning, having been up since three o'clock, was a constant marvel to the groggy ''inmates'' who had put in a full night's sleep and were barely able to stagger to religious services, a requirement of the college for all students. Whether or not the obvious debilitation of some of his friends sparked a bright idea, it was about this time that Jerry thought up another money-making scheme. He had access to all the milk and cream, since he ran the milk through the separator. So he noised it about that he would keep a standing offer of $10 open to any fellow who could drink a quart of thick cream and not regurgitate it. He knew perfectly well that the ability of the human digestive mechanism to tolerate such an assault was impossible. For a couple of years there were no ''takers.''

Finally, though, a student appeared on the scene who could really, in Jerry's words, "stow it away." He appeared to have, instead of a stomach, a bottomless pit. Slyly Jerry kept challenging him, leading him along, softening him up, needling his pride, all in the most subtle, inoffensive way. Sure enough, his victim finally grabbed the bait. Of *course* he could succeed at such a simple project—and he did, through the first half pint, the whole pint, the second half pint and then—*the inevitable!*

For once, Jerry's business sense hadn't been functioning at full capacity. He hadn't taken the precaution of having the drinker put his money on the line. And so all the careful buildup was for nothing, financially speaking, but it did provide much amusement for on-lookers. Also it probably provided Jerry with a great many quiet chuckles. He was never one to guffaw, but rather to savor an incident over and over, wringing every last drop of fun from it.

One summer, instead of working on the farm, he decided that he and a friend could make "a fortune" selling lawn-chairs in an exclusive residential area called Burlingame, south of San Francisco. His reasoning was sound; the chairs were being manufactured at P.U.C. at the lowest possible cost for the precise purpose of sending students out to sell them at a fair profit, thus giving them a chance to get a head start on next year's tuition. Just who originated the idea is not known, but it was a forerunner of many projects of various sorts that have sprung up on the campuses of Adventist colleges, their objectives being the same as those of the lawn-chair enterprise. (It should for the purposes of accuracy be noted, however, that industries in the Seventh-day Adventist school system, one of the strongest parochial systems in America, were completely the rule in the late 1800s and early 1900s, so that the industrial concept was not a new one.)

A colleague, Dr. Merritt Horning, in reflecting on the "lawn-chair episode," says:

"On one occasion we were selling on opposite sides of a residential street in Burlingame. Sales were few and far between and hard to come by. On this particular afternoon I noted Jerry quietly and unusually attentively standing outside a brick backyard wall. Suddenly he disappeared into the yard. I could see only the tops of heads of a group of ladies. I watched and waited anxiously for about twenty minutes, and out Jerry came, beaming with victory. I hurried across the street to hear the story.

24

"A lady was having an afternoon tea in her backyard. Jerry had listened attentively until he heard the hostess excuse herself and go into the house for a brief errand. Whereupon he fearlessly and triumphantly broke into the tea party with his disarming, friendly smile, proceeded to demonstrate our lawn chairs, signed up three orders, and was just preparing to leave when the hostess returned and curtly said, 'What is this?' Jerry, not wishing to press his luck further, spoke kindly to the hostess and made his exit.''

When he and Merritt realized that they weren't even making expenses, they reluctantly decided they'd have to "cut their losses" and return to the farm. Not without one last attempt at city success on Jerry's part, however. Using one of his precious nickels, he bought a newspaper and scanned the want ads.

"Hey, look, Merritt!" he exclaimed excitedly, after a few moments of running his eyes up and down the columns. "This company wants salesmen to sell a meat-tenderizing product. And just look at all their promises—large, fast profits, all sorts of benefits—what do you think?"

"Not much," dryly answered his lawn-chair partner.

Jerry reflected soberly for a few moments. "I agree," was his eventual pronouncement. "Just think of the quantity of that stuff you'd have to sell—tons. It's back to the farm for us," and he jumped to his feet, grabbing for his battered suitcase into which he began stuffing his few clothes.

Each time they saw a Cadillac, Jerry would immediately aver that the driver was undoubtedly a "meat-tenderizer salesman," and kept assuring his friend that without question this would have been their happy luxury had they answered the ad—though of course he believed not one word of his own declaration.

During Jerry's sixteenth year, his father had died in a farm accident. Now, in every way, Jerry must be his own man. Though his mother lived a long, long life, her own death taking place shortly after Jerry's, his relationship with her was not as close as it might have been, probably due in those days to the necessity of his working constantly and to his driving ambition to achieve. His interest in helping his brothers and sister secure an education probably stemmed from his realization that he was the only one left who could do so.

25

Ending of College, Beginning of the Legend / 3

During his last two years of college, Jerry's impact on the institution became ever greater. It is impossible to mention his name to anyone who attended P.U.C. during those years without noticing the face and eyes of the individual light up and hearing that person say, "Do you remember when Jerry—?" Jerry became a Mr. P.U.C. Student Superstar during those years. But his popularity made him no different as a person. If he was aware of his immense personal charisma, he gave no sign of it. He "belonged to the people." A small inner circle thought for years that each was his "best friend"— Charles Anderson, Miriam (Brown) Wood, Kenneth Wood, Milton Lee, Clinton Trott, Vernon Ingle—and it was a bit surprising, though it should not have been, to discover in later years that everyone seemed to feel this way about him.

This is not to say, of course, that he was not entirely human and not above making some mistake, which he preferred that nobody mention. One instance is recounted by the distinguished Dr. Walter Clark, now retired, but for many years Dean of Admissions at the Loma Linda University Medical School. At that time he had not finished his own B.A. degree; he was a young man himself, though married. P.U.C. needed a dean of men. Walter Clark, sufficiently older than the other students, was obviously qualified in every possible way for the job except academically. With some misgivings, he listened as the college president, Dr. W. I. Smith*, during the summer, urged him to function as dean of men while he finished his own B.A. degree.

"We *need* you; God needs you; this is the way it should be," Dr. Smith assured him. And Dr. Smith could be very, very firm, as many students had reason to know, at times to their discomfiture.

---

*Dr. Smith had succeeded W. E. Nelson in 1934.

So two unusual men met under rather unusual circumstances—Jerry Pettis and Walter Clark. Their initial meeting, however, was not exactly auspicious, and probably comes into the category of experiences Jerry preferred to forget. The Seventh-day Adventist Church was having what was then its regular quadrennial world session in San Francisco that spring, for ten days. Of course Jerry was there. He was always where the "action" was. As a matter of fact, he was with Dr. and Mrs. Weniger, who were en route to Washington, D.C. The Seventh-day Adventist Church was just then in the process of setting up what was later to become the Seventh-day Adventist Theological Seminary, and Dr. Weniger was actively involved in this project; Jerry, of course, was his "Man Friday." The Wenigers with Jerry stopped at the meeting in San Francisco.

Just who introduced Walter Clark and Jerry Pettis is not known —but in retrospect it becomes rather clear that Jerry wasn't entirely sure that the correct decision had been made in regard to Walter Clark's future responsibility. He mulled this over and came to one of his clear-cut conclusions. Obviously, he must *advise* the new dean of men, whose academic rank was well below his own.

In tender amusement, Dr. Clark reminisces: "Jerry was the first P.U.C. student I met when I came West. Jerry sought me out and told me he would like to give me some advice as 'an upperclassman.' The advice I have long since forgotten, but I well remember the contact. I was duly impressed. I wasn't entirely clear about his motive, but his confident approach and the fact that he had some positive opinions got my attention, and I came to the conclusion that if he was typical of the fellows I would be living with I was headed for an interesting experience."

But it wasn't all "sweetness and light" when the school year began. These were two strong men. Dean Clark's philosophy on dormitory administration simply did not coincide with Jerry's. So the latter had some hard thinking to do. He was *the* campus student leader. But Dean Clark was in command of the dormitory. What did good sense dictate? One course—he, Jerry, must adjust to the status quo. And he did—so completely and in such a good spirit that Dean Clark asked him to become a "monitor"—a term probably out of the realm of understanding of some modern youth, but these deputies were most important on the various dormitory floors "in those days."

Upper: Jerry (center) with friends Kenneth Wood and Clinton Trott.
Left: Mr. Student P.U.C., and Congressman in the making.
Right: Jerry's birthplace near Phoenix, Arizona.

ENDING OF COLLEGE, BEGINNING OF THE LEGEND

Dr. Clark's perceptions regarding men enabled him to view Jerry accurately.

"As a student Jerry was aggressively involved in campus affairs, and I never found him without an opinion on any issue. I had the impression that championing an unpopular point of view frightened him not in the least; on the contrary, his positive, confident bearing left the impression that he enjoyed a bit of conflict. *Reflecting back, it is not difficult for one to observe his political proclivities surfacing rather early.*"

Who but Jerry Lyle Pettis would conceive and execute the idea of bringing a *cow* into a certain student's room in the men's residence hall? Of course he was always quick to claim that his victim brought it on himself—a rather prim, perfectly behaved young man, who for reasons known only to himself, Jerry felt needed a bit of education not contained in books. The unfortunate student lived on the first floor (though if he had lived on the top floor undoubtedly the outcome would have been no different; Jerry would have figured out a sling and pulley arrangement) so that it was easy for the future congressman, in the middle of a dark night, to select the most docile of his cows, put some sort of harness around the creature's neck, lead it from the barn down to the valley (no small distance)—being careful to avoid the night watchmen—and persuade the bewildered beast to enter the building by the side door. Holding his breath, and counting on the fact that few boys were in the dormitory during the summer, and that they slept like the dead, and that even if they discovered him and his cow, they would say nothing, he made his way down the hall, the cow plodding beside him.

Finally he reached the room of his destination. Cautiously he eased open the door. His "victim" was sleeping the deep sleep of the just and clear-conscienced. Having armed himself with some hay to stuff into the mouth of the bovine animal, to prevent a sudden, melodious "Moo!" from emerging, Jerry maneuvered the cow into the middle of the room, where it stood chewing the hay, an innocent bystander. So the plot unfolded.

Jerry shut the door noiselessly, and stood silently for a moment. Then he began knocking on the room door with all his might.

"Hey, wake up! Wake up!" he yelled at the top of his lungs, throwing open the door, and then sprinting down the hall. He prided himself in athletic events on being one of the fastest runners on the campus. Therefore, he was safely ensconced in the bushes outside the dormitory when the hapless student came to consciousness. Seeing the cow standing in the middle of the room, the moonlight streaming across its glossy coat, he shrieked in terror and disbelief, and promptly leaped from his bed and out the window, running wildly across the campus.

Working with lightning speed (no small feat in dealing with a cow) Jerry had the animal out of the room and secreted in the shrubbery by the time the disoriented and hapless student summoned the courage to return to the dormitory and wake the dean, who was anything but pleased to hear that "there is a cow in my room"—only to find that no evidence existed that such a thing had ever happened.

With his lifelong supply of luck holding, Jerry got the cow back into the barn—undetected—and enjoyed this one joke in strict secrecy. He told no one about it until years later.

His devotion to his church, and his personal commitment to it, began at a very early age and continued to his death. It is no secret, of course, that students in a religious college will have varying interpretations of the doctrines and standards of their church. They will argue and discuss and dissect and even come out with "shockers"— students have always done these things, for this is the time of life when personality is shaping up and an adult philosophy is being formed. Jerry loved long theological discussions, and could almost always convince his opponent that the latter's viewpoint was incorrect, if it differed from his own. He could, though, be pushed too far by what seemed to him irrational statements on the part of "sensationalists."

For one brief period, he roomed with a boy who took great pleasure in announcing to Jerry firmly, "I do *not* believe there is a God!"

Probably the pronouncer was after only one thing—attention. And he got it, in full measure, from J. L. P., who spent time he could ill afford, carefully showing, with good use of the Bible and facts from religion classes, how incredibly wrong the "nonbeliever" was. But the fiercer the discussion raged, the more adamant the "atheist" became.

During one of these sessions, Jerry suddenly took a new tack.

"Then if you don't believe in God, you don't believe in the devil either, of course," he remarked, carefully directing his logic.

The trap was open. The unsuspecting "atheist" walked in, and it snapped shut behind him as he made this declaration: "Well, of course not! There is no such thing as a devil."

Jerry said nothing—a strange type of behavior for him, if only his opponent had had the wit to recognize it. But behind the smooth countenance, the mind was working, planning, organizing. At some time during the day, while his roommate was elsewhere, Jerry secured a large board, and secreted it beneath his bed. The day proceeded on its orderly course. Jerry went to the barn early, but this time he came in again. Never once had his roommate heard him come in, and Jerry was well known for his ability to fall instantly and deeply asleep, when he chose to do so.

Awesome quiet prevailed. Stealthy as a cat, Jerry crept from his bed, got a good grip on the board under his bed, tiptoed to the bed across the room, and delivered a mighty whack on the hindquarters of the innocent sleeper. Quick as a flash and silent as night itself, he reentered his own bed, the board beside him completely covered. Looking upon him, no one would have guessed what had just happened.

Certainly the panicked roommate did not, as he struggled to his feet, groggy and confused.

"Jerry!" he whispered urgently.

No response.

"Jerry, wake up!"

Still no response.

Cautiously, through the narrowest of slits in his eyes, Jerry watched the "unbeliever" rubbing his anatomy and gazing fearfully about the room. Finally he got back into his own bed and eventually his light snoring testified to the conquering of his nerves.

Willing himself to stay awake, in spite of his desperately needed sleep, Jerry crept from his bed again, this time delivering an even more resounding and painful clout to the sleeper. And again he made it to his own bed, undetected.

"Jerry!" called his roommate, too unnerved even to whisper. But he had to keep calling to "wake" the determined sleeper. Finally, though, a muttered, "Wha—is—it?" came forth from the J.L.P. bed.

"Jerry, there's somebody in this room," he whispered fearfully.

"Oh, don't be a nut. Did you wake me up to tell me a fool story like that? Who'd be in here, for Pete's sake? Now let me *sleep*!" When "Pettis" used that particular tone, most people acceded to his requests. The "nonbeliever" was no exception. HE SUBSIDED. And though it took much longer this time, with his anatomy stinging thoroughly, he did eventually get back to sleep.

Now came the third time—the coup de grace. Jerry was able to repeat the incredible performance, undetected. This time, though, his "atheist" was a broken man. Almost in tears, he raced to Jerry's bed and shook him.

"Jerry," he trembled, "there's an evil spirit in this room, and it's been striking me in my sleep. I know it's because I've been saying I don't believe in God or the devil. I'll never say such a thing again, and I want you to remember me in your prayers from now on."

Soothingly, Jerry promised him that he would do that very thing and told him that he was positive, with the erstwhile "atheist" having made this declaration, that there would be no further trouble from the world, the flesh, or the devil. And of course there wasn't— at least, not that kind.

While not highly recommended, young Jerry's method of dealing with doubt was effective, to say the least.

And so the man and the legend grew. The picnic when Jerry and two friends won the "five-legged race" which someone had declared an impossibility, but for which Jerry had programmed two of his friends by much practice. Jerry's well-remembered expression anent public speaking, a field he was determined to challenge and completely master: "I'm going to lay them in the aisles." The year Jerry led the successful campaign for subscriptions to the school paper and then didn't attend the victory banquet (he may not have had the money to buy a corsage for a "date" but would have never admitted it). The year Charles Anderson, Clinton Trott, Kenneth Wood, and Jerry conceived the idea of putting all four beds in one room and their desks in the room across the hall, thus making a "bachelor pad" decades before the term had been coined. The political skill he used in watching his two leading contenders for the presidency of the senior class knock themselves out of the running by their "innocently" nefarious tactics—he picked up the office and the victory with the quiet half-smile of satisfaction that was his hallmark.

One time he spent a weekend in Sacramento with Miller Brockett and his sister, Virginia, where an evangelistic campaign was in progress. Miller, a tenor soloist with a beautiful voice, was to sing for the radio broadcast in conjunction with the address, but suddenly he developed a bad throat. Instantly Jerry volunteered. No mean bass soloist himself, and used to public musical performances, having sung as a member of P.U.C's famous A Cappella Choir for all his college years, under the direction of the late George W. Greer, he saw no problem. One developed, however; he couldn't find the key. The first stanza was terrible. But Jerry wouldn't give up. The second stanza was disaster, but still he persisted. As for the third stanza, the less said, the better. Unfortunately, Dr. Weniger happened to be in the area, caught the broadcast, and was horrified. When Jerry got back on campus, his idol and mentor gave him the "dressing down" of his life. "Never, never accept an appointment without being prepared," Dr. Weniger admonished him. And the counsel took, for Jerry followed it the rest of his life.

And who can forget Jerry's successful master leadership of the campaign to raise funds for a new swimming pool that would replace the mosquito-ridden "pond." Helen and Maurice Mathisen still remember the scene and the exact date, January 12, 1938. The swimming pool campaign reached its goal of $5000 during an assembly, an astronomical sum in those days. Jerry stood in front, handling the audience masterfully, student couriers marching up and down the aisles gathering in the funds. Periodically he would shout out the amount raised. In 58 minutes $1900 was raised to make the campaign a success. That was Jerry, right in there, rousing public opinion, an enthusiastic booster of any worthwhile project.

Note his compassion for a friend who was in even greater financial straits than his own, his meeting of a wealthy man who offered to help Jerry a bit with his bills, and his persuading this gentleman to deposit $250 to the account of his friend also. The friend, who had been told that he would have to leave school if the bill was not paid immediately, might have taken an entirely different turn were it not for this incident. He is now famous and highly successful in his own right, and the $250—via Jerry—will never fade in his memory.

To chronicle all Jerry's romances would take a book in itself. It is doubtful that any girl on campus would not have willingly—eagerly

—dated him. He was circumspect in his relationships, seeming to have plans and opinions about "the fair sex," but wanting to find out about the thinking and reactions and general "makeup" of females. His "Platonic love" was the joke of the campus, as he intended it to be, but he was never a Don Juan. Even those whose hopes of spending the rest of their lives with him were dashed remember him fondly. Some, of course, found him too intense, too highly keyed, too much to live up to. Others sensed incompatibilities that would not make for success in double harness.

He dated constantly—and always had things arranged exactly as he wished—yet it must be noted that dating was, in that particular college in that particular era, surrounded with rigid rules. A couple could not leave the campus to attend a concert or anything else in a nearby town without a chaperon. Certain faculty members were regarded as "better" chaperons than others, for reasons which certainly need not be delineated.

Once, though, Jerry met his match. This was in the large and powerful person of the school physician, Dr. Mary McReynolds, certainly one of the most colorful characters ever to grace a campus. By this time Jerry had managed to secure possession of a beat-up car, and he asked the girl of the moment to attend a concert in San Francisco, a drive of about two hours. Another couple was to share the glorious excursion, a rarity at that time.

"Now, let's see—who will I get for a chaperon?" mused Jerry. Then he thought of Dr. McReynolds—"Dr. Mary" as she was known by all the students. She had made it abundantly clear that Jerry was one of her most favored students. She had been married. She would understand that the turned back of a chaperon enabled a quick hand squeeze or even a light kiss on the cheek of a date or— well, she would understand.

Alas for "the best-laid schemes." When Jerry went to pick up Dr. Mary, for the chaperon must always be picked up first, she calmly positioned herself in the front seat beside him, where she remained for the trip to the concert, sat in the middle of the two young couples during the concert, and sat beside Jerry all the way back. Dr. Mary saw her duty, and she did it. Chaperons must keep young people from temptation, and she aimed to have a clear conscience. It was a pretty crestfallen Jerry who ended the evening.

A romance that might have become serious in his life was the one with Phyllis Kimlin (Dunscombe) who was at P.U.C. only part of a year. Due to her father's death, she returned to Glendale to complete her prenursing and went on into the nurses' course. She and Jerry corresponded, and he visited her in Glendale whenever he could, but her proximity to another young man changed the picture.

Phyllis says, "When I wrote and told Jerry that I had decided to marry Colby, he wrote me back such a beautiful letter. I have kept it through the years, it was so special. I wouldn't want to share it with anyone else, but I do want to share the letter Jerry wrote after my father died."

Angwin, California
April 28, 1934

Dear Phyllis,

Mere words cannot express the feeling I have for your great loss, especially since it was my great privilege to have met your father so recently. I shall never forget his fatherly attitude and counsel which revealed to me a unique character.

I count it a great loss for myself to have lost such a great friend, and believe that my acquaintance with your father makes me understand your bereavement. It is a consolation for us to know that in Christ we have one hope, and that is not far off.

May the words of Revelation 21:4 be a comfort to you, Phyllis. It says there: "God shall wipe away all tears from their eyes; and there shall be no more death, neither sorrow, nor crying, neither shall there be any more pain; for the former things are passed away."

Please accept my heartfelt sympathies for *you* and your family.

Sincerely yours,
Jerry

And so college ended, with Jerry as class president, with the weekend one of glory, and a world waiting for what he had to offer.

Many years later one of his friends would say, "I didn't see Jerry very often, but when I did, we always took up right where we had left off in the past. I remember that whenever a group of us would meet as the years went by, someone would always ask, 'What's Jerry doing now?' He always lived a more exciting life than the rest of us."

The atmosphere of Pacific Union College was deeply spiritual. Jerry was shaped by that atmosphere. It molded and engraved into his character love for God and love for man, integrity, respect for others, and the desire to be of service—qualities that later caused him to become a public servant, though he would have many other kinds of successes in the interim years.

Stanley Folkenberg, a classmate, sums it up poignantly:

"I think of Friday evenings—after vespers, when we fellows would go out for a walk under the stars, and talk about the future. There would be a mixed group, varied from time to time. This is when we expressed our dreams of the future, and when we just sort of opened our hearts there in the dark. I was always impressed with Jerry's determination to succeed, to make something of himself."

P.U.C. from 1933 to 1938 in one sense *was*, from a student's viewpoint, Jerry Pettis. There was no major campaign program, undertaking, class office, or enterprise in which he was not involved. Obviously, it would be impossible to list everything he did, all the offices he held. This list is a sample:

1934–President of The Forum (speech club).

1936–Chairman of committee on plans for father-son banquet.

1936–Summer in Washington, D.C., assisting Dr. Weniger.

1936–1938–Laboratory assistant in Speech for Dr. Weniger.

1934–1938–Bass member and also lector of the A Cappella Choir under the direction of the late George Greer.

1937–Speaker at 20–30 Club in Saint Helena. Topic: His recent trip to Washington, D.C., with Dr. and Mrs. Weniger.

1937–Manager of campaign to raise funds for a new swimming pool.

1937–Winner of oratorical contest sponsored by The Forum.

1937–1938–Occasional feature writer for *Campus Chronicle*, the college newspaper.

1937–President, junior class.

1938–President, senior class.

INTERLUDE OF SORROW

In the summer of 1937, between his junior and senior years of college, Jerry married—a marriage at first kept secret, but which soon became known. The marriage lasted for about eight years.

What can be said that is fair to both the living and the dead? "The moving finger writes, and having writ, moves on." When people are very young, and physical attraction is strong, couples are often blinded to the fact that their goals and values and aspirations lead in different directions.

But scars and wounds are left, inevitably.

Jerry's first child, Yvonne, was born to this marriage.

Minister, Teacher, Aviator /4

In the several months preceding his graduation in 1938 with a B.A. degree in speech, Jerry began to do some really hard thinking about his future—the practical side of the future. It is one thing to want to "succeed" and to be willing to put your "all" into your work —but *what* work? A speech degree does not qualify a man for many openings other than the teaching of this subject—and in that era, speech was not a large department in any college. Few, if any, openings existed. The Seventh-day Adventist Church was a highly conservative organization in its attitude at that time toward acceptable professions for its members. And the one profession which Jerry had a burning desire to embrace was closed to him by the attitude of the church. More than anything else, he wished to be a lawyer.

This is not the appropriate place to discuss the reasons for the attitude of the church—an attitude which has since changed drastically. But one lives life where his life is, in the space-time continuum. (A little-known fact about Jerry, however, is that later on in his life he actually took a law course by correspondence, and passed all the tests with no difficulty, but never sat for his bar examinations. However, the knowledge he gained would prove immensely useful to him in later years as a businessman and legislator.)

Because of his leadership ability and tremendous speaking talents, it should have come as no surprise to the campus when presidents of local conferences of the church in the area known as the Pacific Union Conference—which comprised all of California, Arizona, Utah, and Nevada—began to view Jerry with great interest. Sad to say, however, not all the theology majors were as elated as their profession of love for their fellowman should have caused them to be when various presidents made trips to P.U.C. to interview this young speech major with definite employment in their minds.

To be charitable to them, however, it should be pointed out that the theology and religion majors made up a great share of the graduating class, since the church at that time held that the organized denominational setup had to be staffed by the products of the few Seventh-day Adventist colleges throughout North America. There was just one small problem—the Depression had still not fully released its grip on America, and so the competition (Christian, of course!) for "ministerial internships" was keen.

To give experience to the fledgling preachers, the teachers in the religion departments always had a small evangelistic "effort" going somewhere in one of the surrounding small towns, such as Calistoga, Yountville, Santa Rosa, Vacaville, Pope Valley—wherever they could secure a "hall" (often just a room) and advertise, mostly by word of mouth, that religious meetings, free to everyone, would be held each Sunday night. The religion and theology majors suffered much anguish as they prepared their sermons, most of them doctrinal in content, and delivered them in the presence of their own experienced teachers who certainly must have suffered equally at some of the inept attempts they were forced to sit through.

Jerry, though, had undergone none of these tortures of the body, soul, and spirit. Though he had taken a very active part in the religious activities of the college, he was not connected with the religion department.

Then it came—an invitation, a bona fide offer, a "call," in the parlance of the church, to become a ministerial intern in—Arizona! It is interesting to speculate as to what his answer would have been if the call had been to another location. But the very word "Arizona" evoked all those images of wide open spaces and purple desert, and sagebrush and ranches and—well, he and Arizona understood each other.

But he did not have one formal sermon in his possession, a rather formidable drawback for a young man entering the ministry. So he counseled with at least one other member of the class, John Baerg, an older member who had returned to college to finish his degree, though he had been in the ministry for several years prior to this.

"John," Jerry asked him, with that intense gaze which he used in discussing matters of the gravest importance, "Do you think I should enter the ministry?"

Not for one moment did John hesitate. He had a conviction.

"I think there is no question whatsoever that this is what you should do. I believe with all my heart that the Lord is leading you in this direction. I think that your place is in public evangelism. That's where you belong."

Reassured, Jerry told John that his mind was almost made up—and a few days later he came and said, "John, I'm going to do it. I'll have lots of work ahead of me in Bible study, but with God's help, I think I can make it."

Then he set about mending his fences with the religion majors, convincing them that nobody in the world but J. L. Pettis would want to go to the "wilds" of Arizona. Before long, teachers and students alike in the department were scurrying in all directions to prepare Jerry with enough sermon material so that he could manage at least for the first few months. Though he did not follow the calling of the ministry very long, the knowledge he gained of the organization of the church, and his interest in its workings were to remain with him forever. To the day of his death, he could preach a powerful sermon.

But there wasn't much to indicate the future when he and his wife pulled into the dusty little town of Kingman, Arizona, all the happy college days over. If ever it was true that "The shouting and the tumult dies; the captains and the kings depart"—it was true now. Real, hard, tough, down-to-earth life must be lived, on the magnificent sum of $18 per week. Moreover he must "prove his calling," a popular expression among evangelical churches of that era, which, translated, meant that a young man must be able to do anything asked of him, from pitching a tent, to debating doctrines with the most accomplished theologian in the town—and make his paycheck stretch over the entire month. But Jerry lived on challenges.

The president of the Arizona Conference of Seventh-day Adventists plotted out Jerry's immediate work for him.

"I'm giving you a good singer to help with the music," he announced as Jerry sat groping about for a "handle" in the new situation. "You and he will pitch a small tent, and you'll hold a series of meetings. You'll be responsible for the entire endeavor, the sermons, the advertising, balancing the budget, being sure that the tent is safe night and day—in other words, you're 'it.' "

"Well," thought Jerry, "it doesn't sound so different from campaigns I've run in college, but of course there'll be a new sermon every night (it was customary to hold these meetings Sunday through Thursday nights) and in college I had only myself to think about. Now I have a wife and will soon have a baby—but I can do it! I know I can!''

And so the future United States Congressman found himself five nights a week preaching to a crowd that averaged between six and twelve, most of them either Indians or cowboys with nothing better to do. The tiny town of Kingman wasn't much interested in religion; even Jerry's eloquence couldn't change that. Before long, the singing assistant was sent to a new assignment, and Jerry was alone with his work.

After you have visited all the church members—when perhaps there are twenty of those, and tried to visit the people attending your meetings, if you can dig them out of the saloons and off the reservations—all six of them—and after you have prepared your sermon for the night, what do you do with yourself, when you're more or less camping in a little adobe house?

But the Pettis inventiveness could never be safely underestimated. Jerry reasoned that what he most needed was to get acquainted in the town. People needed to know he was *there*. He needed to find a way to meet them on *their* ground—then perhaps they'd be willing to come and meet him on *his*.

As in many small towns, Kingman had a community baseball team, the pride of the citizens. Confident as always of his ability to pull it off, Jerry approached the manager about being given a place on the team. Taken aback, the sun-grizzled, taciturn desert man looked him over.

"Well," he drawled, "let's see what you can do."

Jerry could do it all—hit, catch, field, grab "sizzling grounders," run, slide—the works.

The manager assured him that he was from then on a team member.

Truth *is* stranger than fiction; writers have always known this. In the life of Jerry Pettis, though, if facts were not verifiable, a biographer might be accused of constructing incidents out of "whole cloth." Nevertheless, who but Jerry Pettis would be at bat during the most crucial game of the year, the game with Las Vegas? Who but Jerry would be the *last* man at bat, with two men on base? And who but Jerry would belt out a home run which won the game, causing all of Kingman to go wild with exultation? And who but Jerry would find himself written up in the local newspaper as the hero of the decade? And who but Jerry would have caught the attention of the sports desk of United Press in nearby Phoenix, so that the story of the "ball-playing preacher" was sent out over all the wire services?

Almost the first person to see the story in the Phoenix paper was the conference president. He paled visibly. What in the world was going on with that young man over in Kingman? After all, the proper role of an evangelist was— He decided the only thing to do was to drop everything, drive to Kingman, and give some badly needed instruction to the young hopeful. "Ball-playing preacher," indeed!

When the conference executive walked into the tent, just as the service was beginning, he found more than 200 people crowded there —standing all around the sides. Wall-to-wall people, all of them wanting to hear the "ball-playing preacher."

In today's world, Jerry's escapade seems no escapade at all. Preachers are *expected* to be normal human beings. But in that particular era, one must remember, the general concept defined three sexes—men, women, and clergymen.

It was during his first year at college, 1933–34, that Jerry had confirmed his lifelong love affair with flying. About seven miles away lived a farmer, Bill Eddy, who had an airplane. Jerry talked the farmer into giving him lessons. In exchange, he would work so many hours in return, in addition to his work at the college. As regularly as he could, the sixteen-year-old would hitchhike to the farm.

The lessons continued until the college president heard about them. Dr. Nelson worried that Jerry might get hurt and that the college would bear the blame. He gave the young man a choice—college or flying. Jerry chose college.

But the next year there came a new college president, one who wasn't so worried about airplanes as his predecessor had been. Soon, the young man was back, thumbing his way to the sky.

Though his declaration, "Someday I'm going to be a pilot!" made at the Arizona State Fair several years before, had had to be put aside temporarily, he decided the time had come, after the P.U.C. flying lessons. To this day it is unclear how he managed to pay for the flying lessons which he then embarked upon. One suspects that he traded various kinds of favors with the pilot of the plane in Kingman and other small towns where he picked up lessons.

He was born to fly. He seemed not to need the lessons. He seemed to have met his natural habitat, the sky. And he obtained his pilot's license, to the utter stupefaction of his more myopic friends. America at that time, in general, had not yet fully accepted aviation.

"The airplane will change the entire world in just a few years," Jerry told friend after friend. "Man, it's inevitable. Just look what it will mean in the way of quick transportation, commerce, national defense—why, there's not any area of living that won't be affected by flying."

The full-to-bursting tent in that country town was not a one-time-only phenomenon. People came and stayed. There were other towns and other meetings, and finally, there was "the big city," Phoenix, where Jerry met another of the men who would have a profound impact upon his life. This was the distinguished H. M. S. Richards, himself a man of unusual vision, another man of "firsts." Peerless speaker and evangelist, he had grasped the incredible magnitude of the effect the radio could have upon the religious life of America and, with mountains of faith and a molehill of money, in the early 30s had pioneered "The Voice of Prophecy" program, which has been an active part of American radio life ever since.

Pastor Richards, in addition to his radio program, aired live weekly, was expected to conduct a large series of meetings throughout the Pacific Union Conference. To work with him through such a series was the dream of every young preacher. Jerry was assigned to this giant of a man, who had the deep perception to realize in a few short weeks that his "intern" was no run-of-the-mill, plodding young preacher.

Throughout their lifetime they would remain close. Later, after Jerry's first marriage had crumbled, Pastor Richards would officiate at his marriage to Shirley one singing golden day—and a generation later he would officiate at the funeral of the United States Congressman on a day of bleakness and despair.

Dr. Richards says today: "Jerry filled his place in life with grace and efficiency. I believe he could have occupied any place of responsibility this country has to offer. And he had a superb and saving gift of humor.

"I knew something about his faith in God. I've been close to him when he met discouragement, heartbreak, success. Brilliant—talented —he was many things. Best of all, he was a man, a real man.''

If Dr. Richards affected Jerry profoundly, the reverse also is true. Frankly, Dr. Richards confesses, ''I do not think I would ever have had the courage to fly anywhere if it had not been for Jerry. I was holding a series of tent meetings in Phoenix when he introduced me to the retired military pilot who was then continuing his [Jerry's] lessons. Jerry did not say much, but I decided that while I was afraid to go into the air, for the sake of God's cause I'd better get used to it. The pilot took me up in a plane with double controls and let me guide the plane around over the city of Phoenix, and over the very tent where I preached every night.

''When we came back near the airport, he told me I must land the plane. He said to think of it simply as going downhill and to keep it going about 60 miles per hour. I've never had my hands on the controls of a plane since, but I've flown all over the world and around it more than once.''

Another meaningful ''first'' for Jerry—and an impact on the destiny of a man who has himself influenced the destiny of tens of thousands.

Then the Richards's meetings were over, and the tiny, dusty Arizona towns loomed up again—but not for J. L. P. His star was on the ascendancy in the Seventh-day Adventist Church. Never was the biblical text more true that ''a man's gift maketh room for him.'' Another outstanding evangelist, Fordyce Detamore, was located in Kansas City, Missouri—crowds were flocking to hear him—and though he had a staff of assistants, he needed ''just the right person.'' His friend and mentor, H. M. S. Richards, when asked to recommend who this should be, replied instantly, ''Jerry Pettis.''

Another move—''Go East,'' young man of the West. His association with the dynamic Fordyce Detamore, and later, with Evangelist Lylon Lindbeck increased Jerry's already notable pulpit skills.

But outstanding evangelists were rare, and administrators of the church felt that Pastor Detamore should move on to Omaha. Who would watch over the fledgling members in the Kansas City Metropolitan Church? Who would give them the loving attention and care that new church members must have if they are to grow and flourish? Jerry Pettis.

At that time, for such a young man to take up the pastorate of a large city church was remarkable.

"He was fun to work with," Fordyce Detamore recalls. "Our paths didn't cross very often as the years came and went; but finally, we came face to face at a service honoring forty years of radio evangelism by H. M. S. Richards. I had been the latter's associate in the early radio days. Jerry and I lunged at each other, and out of both our mouths came the same words, 'There you are, you old rascal!' "

In just two and a half years, under the Pettis pastoring, the church grew from 380 to nearly 800 members.

But we must not overlook another "first." Together, Jerry Pettis and Fordyce Detamore established one of the first Seventh-day Adventist Bible correspondence schools. Today Bible correspondence schools are conducted all over the world, and are considered to be a major factor in the evangelistic outreach of the church.

At one point, the Detamore evangelistic company left Kansas City to hold a short series of meetings in a small nearby town. Since it was of such short duration, the entire company were housed in a small hotel, most of them in the same corridor. Jerry's wife was not with him, though most of the other wives were along. Pastor Detamore distinctly remembers an incident that Jerry emphatically did not wish to be reminded of.

After one of the night meetings, Jerry had stayed later than usual, talking to the interested members of the audience. Then he went for a brisk walk through the little town, convinced that he must have exercise. (He was always an "exercise nut," long before the medical profession became so vocal on this subject.) All these activities brought him into the little hotel quite late. All was quiet—the corridor was only dimly lighted. Down the hall he tiptoed and into his room.

Not bothering to turn on the light, he stripped down to his shorts (having first visited the communal men's room at the end of the hall) and, with a huge bound, cleared the foot of the bed and landed with a crash into—a bed occupied by the wife of one of the other members of the evangelistic company! In the dark and in his preoccupation he had entered the wrong room. The bloodcurdling shriek of the bed's occupant nearly froze his blood—but it is rumored that a faster exit was never achieved by anyone anywhere.

Fate always seemed to be peeking around the corners of Jerry's life, holding in its hands unsuspected opportunities, unexpected challenges. Therefore, it should have come as no surprise that, though no openings for speech teachers seemed available when he graduated from college, almost as soon as he arrived in Kansas City, Union College, in Lincoln, Nebraska, was in desperate need of just such a person. This Adventist college serves all the Midwest, and it had to be staffed. Negotiations began between the administration of the college and the administration of the local conference, Jerry's employers.

"Why, it's out of the question!" the conference administrators exploded. "Do you realize that Union College is about 200 miles from Kansas City? Just how can this young man contribute to the work of the church here and teach speech classes at Union College?"

Jerry was called in on the problem. He needed the exhilaration of living on an "impossible" schedule. Without it he was only half-alive. And so he came up with a characteristic plan.

All the speech classes could be scheduled for Mondays and Tuesdays. He would catch the midnight train in Kansas City on Sunday night, ride to Lincoln, Nebraska, and arrive at 6 a.m., just one hour before his first scheduled class. Then, after his last class, about noon on Tuesday, he would catch the train back, arriving just in time for the night meeting. The conference and the college would each contribute to his magnificent salary (about $25 per week)—and Union College would pay his transportation.

Unbelievingly, the administrators looked him up and down.

"Nobody can live on a routine like that!" they announced firmly. "It means you will miss one full night's sleep each week. You won't be any good to either job. It's out of the question."

Jerry never needed his gift of diplomacy more than at this moment. After all, when you're just getting started, and scrambling for a foothold in the "real" world, you can't afford to offend the people who have power to influence your destiny.

He quietly asked, "Would you be willing to let me try it for a month? If either party to the arrangement is unhappy with it, then I'll bow out of the teaching."

Undoubtedly the administrators were sure that Jerry would "learn his lesson" and come crawling to them a month later, begging for both sympathy and release. Then he would get his well-deserved lecture.

That lecture still remains in the archives of undelivered orations. For at least one year Jerry lived on that routine, neglecting neither job, performing brilliantly on both, and loving every minute of it. Later on, he began flying back and forth, which reduced the physical strain on him considerably. He had become, in addition to everything else, a flying instructor in an aviation program in Kansas. So now, in addition to being "the ball-playing preacher" he was "the flying preacher," and it was not at all uncommon for him to drop in from the sky on some of the other pastors in the state.

His relationships with Pastor Richards and Pastor Detamore, radio pioneers, had also developed his interest in that media, so that he kept a radio program going all the time he was pastoring in Kansas City. Jerry's days always had a large component of elastic in them, according to his bewildered friends and observers.

Union College, however, liked him so well, and the students responded so enthusiastically to his dynamic personality that they began putting intense pressure on him to become a full-time faculty member.

"You can make just as great a contribution to the church teaching young people as you can preaching," they told him. "In fact, you may even make a greater, for you will be training others in the kinds of approaches you believe in. Come and be one of us!"

Decision time again. Factor weighing time.

"Yes, I believe that at this point God is leading me in the direction of teaching," he told the elated Union College administrators and the crestfallen conference officials. "But there's just one thing. I will need to get an M.A. immediately. My B.A. degree is simply not enough for college teaching."

"No problem!" declared the happy college president. "You can enroll at the University and get your M.A. while you're teaching. We'll foot the bill, of course."

And he did get the M.A. He taught full-time, took full work at the University, and had his M.A. within a year and a half.

One student from those days says, "He had a profound effect upon my life. I can never forget him. He was the one teacher who gave me a vision of what I could accomplish if I set my goals high enough."

Dunbar Smith, then a pastor in Omaha, now a physician, recalls

Jerry's youthful prophecy concerning the importance of aviation in the future of America and the world comes true, and Jerry grows along with the wave of the future.

that Jerry took on an added responsibility—that of helping pastors in the Middle West with their speech problems. "I had been a missionary in India, and when I returned, I had a voice difficulty," he says. "Jerry actually took the time to come and monitor my sermons to see if he could suggest some way to solve the problem."

James J. Aitken, an official of the General Conference of Seventh-day Adventists, formerly liaison officer with Congress, who knew Jerry well, sums up his contribution during his years at Union College:

"He knew what articulate delivery in speech meant to a man in public. He gave Union College a wonderful insight into just what proper speech training could mean to young men and women."

But the bright clouds over his professional career were becoming obscured by the dark clouds over his personal life. It became clear that changes would have to be made; personality clashes in the home were striking deep. After much prayer and counsel with others, a sorrowful Jerry knew that he must leave campus life in the Middle West. His problems were understood by the administrators of the college and the various conferences; perhaps a change of work and scene would solve what seemed unsolvable.

And so it was arranged that Jerry should return to the ministry in Denver, Colorado. But by this time World War II had broken out. The United States had entered the most desperate struggle of its history. Jerry had strong convictions about serving his country, and he engaged in the desperate race to train sufficient pilots to defend the free world against aggressors. (History has documented the ill-preparedness of this nation, and the incredible blindness of some national leaders at that point.)

For a short time Jerry pastored a church in Denver. Then he volunteered, on a part-time basis, to serve as a flying instructor—"the flying parson," his students had called him. And it became clear to him that his duty, as he saw it, was to ask for a leave of absence from his position with the church in order to give his talents to his sorely beset country. This was granted. While he was still in Denver, he headed the Search and Rescue Group of the Second Air Force.

Jerry became a pilot for the Air Transport Command, under contract to United Airlines. He flew countless dangerous missions to the South Pacific, piloting cargo planes from 1944 to 1946, and flying military and government personnel to those areas.

49

NASA AIR FORCE PHOTOS

Finally the bitter war years ended. But other things had ended for Jerry also. His marriage. For this man who had never known defeat, the years ahead looked bleak. His friends, scattered all over the globe, did their best to encourage the man who had spent his life encouraging others.

"Someday you will be happy again," they told him.

Secretly, he wondered.

Professionally, though, he had decided to make aviation his life. Not only did he fly over the Pacific for United Airlines, he became, finally, assistant to the president of the company.

EXPLOSION OF JOY

Running like a dark thread through all his professional successes, the sustained tensions of the war years, and the constant career flying afterward, was his personal loneliness. Based in San Francisco, whenever he found it possible Jerry visited P.U.C., able to recapture for a "few brief, shining moments" the happiness and promise of those student years. The year 1946–47 was Dr. Weniger's last year as chairman of the speech department; he would move to Washington, D.C., the next summer to become dean of the Seventh-day Adventist Theological Seminary. But for now Jerry found comfort and solace in his company.

Another close friend was Dr. Richard Lewis, who, during Jerry's student days, had been principal of the preparatory school on the college campus and had now returned, with his Stanford doctorate, as a teacher in both the speech and English departments. Richard and his wife Virginia were determined that things had to come out right for Jerry—anything else was unthinkable.

Almost out of the blue, Dr. Weniger, who knew that Dr. Lewis was looking for a secretary-assistant, asked him, "Have you met Shirley McCumber McNulty? She's already a college graduate, you know, but her young doctor husband died out in the Pacific during the war. Now she's here taking prenursing, getting her life started all over again. Would you like to meet her?"

Dr. Lewis met her. And he *knew*. And Virginia met her. And *she* knew. But they were much too intelligent to approach this kind of delicate situation carelessly. Here were two mature young adults, both hurt by life, frontally. Very, very casually, they arranged a

"Sabbath dinner" for the next time Jerry would visit P.U.C. Shirley regarded the dinner invitation as an act of gracious courtesy on the part of her boss.

There is no verifiable record that time stood still for a breathtaking moment when Dr. Lewis said, "Shirley, I'd like you to meet Jerry." But Jerry always thought of that moment as suspended in time, encapsulated in crystal prisms. He, the eloquent, the charmer, the sophisticate, the world traveler, the self-assured, was speechless—dazzled then and ever afterward by the girl standing before him.

She was tall and slender, and graceful as a willow in the wind. Shining auburn hair, eyes the bluest Jerry had ever seen, skin the clearest and creamiest, teeth the most sparkling, legs sheer perfection—surely, if ever there was "a vision of delight" it was Shirley.

But she was so much more than that. She was the product of the marriage of two brilliant personalities, their only child, on whom they had lavished all their dreams and hopes, never spoiling her, but nurturing her quick, incisive mind, her inquiring interest in all things. Her father, Dr. Harold McCumber, was one of the most outstanding history teachers of the Seventh-day Adventist Church, as his students in "Western Civilization" will testify. The very flower of Western civilization—Shirley. Though she had suffered anguish deeper than she had believed possible, the courage that was even then one of her most outstanding attributes had taken over. She would start life anew.

It was a meeting of two indomitable spirits, two people of very special quality, two larger-than-life personalities.

They were married on March 2, 1947.

Shirley would become his lover and best friend, a brilliant conversationalist and gracious hostess, devoted mother of his children, an accomplished public speaker, his companion in world travel, and eventually his political partner, campaigning shoulder to shoulder with him, never complaining that, as the years went on, she had less and less of him, as his country had more and more.

Jerry had found his "someday."

Businessman / 5

Jerry would retain a lifetime interest in aviation, always keeping a private pilot's license.* He also retained a commercial license (United Airlines issued him a special gold license which he carried in his wallet) but it was time, his mental clock told him, to explore new fields. Life was glorious. He and Shirley, with their boundless enthusiasm for living, greeted each new day with the absolute conviction that this would be the best day of their lives. And each one was. Later on, there were Peter and Debbie, giving added meaning and dimension to living.

For now, though, Jerry began to realize that he had two overwhelming interests—one of them which he had always realized, and the other relatively new and unexplored. The first, public relations. The second, business—the world of finance, corporations, and invention. That harness strapped to the back of the cow on the Arizona ranch, which he had devised when he was fourteen, was only a forerunner of the practical, marketable projects he would originate.

His first move, though, was a kind of double-headed approach, in that he was asked to become business manager of the Alumni Association of what would become Loma Linda University, in Loma Linda, California, at that time exclusively a medical college. (He was intimately associated with this institution for the rest of his life, later functioning for several years as vice-president for development.) When he became business manager on January 1, 1947, his concept of the work was completely innovative. The traditional tight-fisted "Come on, alumni, fork over your money for your dear old alma mater" was not for him. Immediately he familiarized himself with the problems of the job, and the needs from the business angle. But he also saw his role as that of a public-relations expert.

---

*For instance, he was a charter member of the *Sky Roamers* at Burbank Lockheed Airport, one of the largest private flying clubs in the world, established in 1950.

"After all," he would say, "if you're trying to get people to support ideas and projects, you have to sell yourself first." No problem there. During the three and a half years that he functioned in this role, he introduced so many program changes that the association still regards him as something of a "patron saint." He was all over the United States, and the world, visiting the alumni, his beautiful wife with him whenever possible.

When Jerry opened the first "official" Alumni Association office, his first project was to organize alumni chapters. He flew back and forth across the U.S. meeting with alumni, church leaders, and anyone else who could be helpful. During his first year, he traveled 100,000 miles by air, and visited personally with 500 alumni in their homes and offices.

Seeking to augment the effectiveness of the Alumni Association, he became an associate editor of the *Alumni Journal,* helped to expand its publication, and solicited display advertising to help defray publication costs. Though it had been the custom to list opportunities for physicians here and there throughout the journal, Jerry developed the plan of organizing this service into a real "placement" bureau and employed a placement secretary to give greater service to the members.

Always interested in scholastic and academic excellence, Jerry encouraged the alumni members to secure publication of their scientific articles in prominent medical journals, thus bringing greater prestige to the medical school. He also joined in promoting the establishing of a school of dentistry at Loma Linda University, a dream which later was realized.

In 1947 he inaugurated the first "Alumnus of the Year" award and the "Honored Alumnus" award. Fittingly enough, in 1972 he became the first recipient of the Alumni Association's "Distinguished Service Award."

With Jerry, one thing always led to another and bigger thing. He began mulling one such project over in his mind. Why not establish his own public relations firm? He familiarized himself with every aspect of this kind of work; cannily he secured legal counsel on the finer points of corporations and law (though previously he had taken his law course by correspondence and was very well informed) and on the probable capital needed for a beginning.

Shirley, whose confidence in his ability was unlimited, couldn't wait for the new venture to get started. Her face lighted up with anticipation.

"I think it's a terrific idea!" she declared. "Let's go!"

And so in 1950 he established his own public relations firm, Jerry Pettis and Associates, probably wondering privately just how many clients he would attract. (At the same time he continued his work with the Alumni Association of the university for another year.)

The firm was an overwhelming success, especially in the medical field. His clients included the California Medical Association and the Los Angeles County Medical Association. In fact, the latter organization was so pleased with his approach to their problems and needs that later he became "special assistant to the president"—not just the public relations expert.

At about this time, a close friendship was established between Jerry and Shirley and Bob and Marguerite Marsh. Bob was a young surgeon in Glendale, California. Their rapport was instantaneous. The four of them shared a love of adventure, of travel, and of flying. Through the years, they spent as much time together as their crowded lives would permit—but they, young and eager and peering expectantly into the future, could never have known then that on one soft California day, Bob would serve as a pallbearer at his best friend's funeral. How gracious of the Creator not to allow men to know the disappointments of the future! (As a matter of fact, these couples shared a "second generation" friendship, since Bob's father and Shirley's father had been roommates as students at Union College, in Nebraska.)

Among Jerry's most interesting clients were several well-known medical television shows. He served as technical consultant for *Ben Casey, Dr. Kildare,* and *Hennessey,* calling upon Dr. Bob Marsh and others to gather the medical counsel needed for production. Eventually he formed a committee to provide consultation service to the various motion picture and television industry producers who were making medically oriented films.

"How in the world do you know so much about medicine?" someone asked him after he'd pointed out glaring inconsistencies in a script about to be filmed.

He looked up, surprised. "Well, you can hardly spend all the

In the international outreach of the Loma Linda University heart team to Pakistan, Greece, Viet Nam, and the far-flung reaches of earth, Jerry, second from right, lends his public relations expertise. As a result of this goodwill, Loma Linda University and America have become synonyms of hope and healing throughout the world.

time I have spent with the medical profession and not learn *something!*" he twinkled.

One of his college classmates, home on furlough from the mission field, visited Jerry in his public relations office during those years. During that time, the Seventh-day Adventist Church had not yet seen the importance of good "P.R."—and this bothered Jerry enormously, since he always considered the fate of his church inextricably bound up with his own.

"Jerry was outspoken and definitive as to how the church could present a better picture of itself to the community and the world," recalls his classmate. "And he was impatient with the slow way things moved, the necessity to get everything voted by one committee after another. He felt that it was almost criminal to waste opportunities and talents."

He didn't waste anything. In addition to all his other activities, he became a founding member of the Public Relations Society of America. He helped formulate its first code of ethics. As a matter of fact, he functioned as one of the officers of the newly born organization, just to be sure that it would get a good start.

And now, from the chrysalis of the public relations expert began to emerge the businessman. The boy who had taken charge of his life at 14, financed almost his entire education, offered $10.00 to anyone who could drink and retain a quart of cream, who had wrested flying lessons out of an impossible $18 per week salary, became a man wide-awake to potentials and possibilities at that time undreamed of by others.

Since his work with the medical profession was so close, he had begun to understand what an enormous amount of time a physician must consume in reading medical journals just to keep himself informed of what is going on in his world. A doctor must be up-to-date. He must know the latest treatments, the newest drugs, the most recent findings—he must keep abreast. (This aspect of medicine is not always understood by the layman.) But Jerry heard the despairing remark from his scores of physician friends constantly—"I just can't find the time to do the reading I have to do!"

An idea struck him. Why not put articles from all the outstanding medical journals on tape? Then, as a physician rode in his car, he could always be listening to professional material. He need not waste any travel time. Instead, it would be "learning time." Jerry could hardly wait to discuss his idea with Shirley.

As always, she was with him all the way. "It's the best idea I think I've ever heard!" was her pronouncement. Her confidence was reassuring; he knew that she had a keen mind. Large risks would be involved; money would have to be borrowed to get the project started. Realist that he was, Jerry knew that there is always an "iffy" quality in a completely new concept. How will it be received? He cautiously discussed it with some of his physician friends—and, as might have been expected, the less visionary were unenthusiastic. Who in the world ever heard of listening to medical articles on tapes in a car? (One must remember that the whole audio-visual concept of learning in every area has changed since about 1953, when Jerry got his idea.)

Others, though, received the idea enthusiastically.

"We always felt," says Bob Marsh, "that the final *decision* to go ahead with the project was made in our living room, after the four of us had discussed for the last time every possible angle."

"All right, let's go ahead with it," Jerry said.

"But what will you call the tape service?" Shirley asked him.

He thought for a moment.

"The Audio-Digest," he replied confidently. And that is what it became.

Initially, medical articles were merely read into a microphone. Jerry secured the services of an electronics technician who had recently migrated to this country from Europe. Cliff Whenmuth would copy the tapes from one master machine onto half a dozen tape recorders. In the infancy of this kind of thing, he had to change tapes every half hour, because the re-recording was done at standard speed. And of course there were the packaging and the marketing and—everything that goes into this kind of project. The details were so numerous that even yet Shirley shudders when she thinks of it. Her services were commandeered, even to helping with the tapes and with the packaging.

"Why in the *world* can't some company in the duplicating field come up with a high-speed duplicator?" Jerry fumed, over and over, as the laborious process of duplicating went on, with tapes to be changed each half hour.

He didn't just fume, though. He induced Ampex to develop a high-speed duplicating unit. But this came somewhat later.

It's one thing to produce a product. It's another thing to let people know that the product is available. With his capital tied up in the tapes themselves, Jerry sat down to figure out how this could be accomplished.

"Shirley, you'll simply have to go to as many doctors' offices as possible and show them the Audio-Digest and sell them the idea," he told her.

For once, Shirley was stupefied.

"Like a door-to-door salesman?" she asked weakly.

"Exactly!" was his uncompromising rejoinder.

As it turned out, not only did the beautiful Shirley become a "door-to-door salesman," but so did her parents, Dr. and Mrs. McCumber, who by that time had retired and moved to California. And they were *successful*. Subscriptions began to pour in.

Jerry had done his "homework" carefully, in securing as his first editor a man whose name had become famous in American medical circles—Dr. Edward Rosonow, later executive director of the American Board of Internal Medicine. This busy doctor selected and condensed and edited the articles and recorded many of them. Other pressing duties forced him to bow out of the Audio-Digest after a time, but by then it was a huge enterprise.

Always a shrewd judge of men, Jerry asked the vivid and talented Claron Oakley to become the next editor. Claron had university degrees in radio and television and shared Jerry's enthusiasm. By this time, Shirley had graduated from her door-to-door salesman's role, but she and Claron's wife Julie Oakley attended every medical convention possible, selling the idea to groups. Surely the most dedicated women's libber will not object to the observation that, with two beautiful, determined women as *salespeople*, the company had a built-in "secret weapon."

The company was proliferating so rapidly, so many new aspects were being developed, that Jerry knew he must make some decisions. He had already hired his *own* public relations man—after all, even he couldn't function in *every* capacity! After consultations with board members and stockholders, it was decided to split Audio-Digest into editorial function and tape-duplicating function. The editorial area was given to the California Medical Association. Jerry remained in this part of the organization as a vice-president.

On the tape-duplicating side, he and Cliff Whenmuth became partners, retaining the tape-duplicating business and forming a new company called Magnetic Tape Duplicators. Eventually this organization would become the world's largest user and duplicator of magnetic recording tape.

Having invested his returns carefully, Jerry now turned more capital into the business. Other accounts poured in; Audio-Digest became only one of the projects. When Jerry sold the company, it brought over two million dollars.

Characteristically, Jerry arranged that the proceeds from part of the sale would continue to furnish scholarships for medical sudents who could find no other way to secure their training. He set up a non-profit organization, which has contributed more than a million dollars for medical education.

Claron Oakley, now vice-president of Audio-Digest, and executive editor of "Audio-Digest Reporter," found Jerry an amazement throughout the remainder of their lives together.

"Early in our relationship," says Claron, "I thought: Is this guy putting me on? Bring up *any* subject—sow belly commodity futures, flora and fauna of the Okefenokee swamp, the composition of the Andromeda galaxy, ad infinitum—and he seemed to know more about it than *Encyclopaedia Britannica* or the scriptwriters for *Information Please*. The simple fact was, however, that no matter how glib and informed he sounded, he really *was* informed. Like some infallible I.R.S. computer, his fertile brain recorded and stored everything he heard or read, just waiting to spew it all back out at some appropriate moment in future conversation or debate."

Jerry need fear poverty no more. Though he boasted to the end of his life that he could milk a cow with the best of them, he would never need to prove it. He owned a private plane; he flew it everywhere in the States. He and the Oakleys and the Marshes and other friends were often on world tours, visiting every exotic spot on the globe. But as soon as he had seen it, he was ready to go again. Shirley knew that she had better be ready to repack within twenty-four hours of any landing, anywhere.

Once she wailed to her mother, in a rare moment of fatigue, "I wonder how I will ever keep up with him!''

Her witty and lovely mother replied dryly, ''Well, when you've latched onto the tail of a comet, you're bound to have some uncomfortable moments!''

Flying his plane, Jerry was totally calm, with nerves of steel and judgment of perfection when actual disaster threatened. Knowing this, few of his close friends have been able to accept the ''pilot error'' verdict regarding his death. There were so many emergencies he coped with—for instance, once, high over the desolate desert of Texas, one of the plane doors suddenly blew open, and the incoming rush of wind threatening to suck all the occupants into the sky.

''Close it,'' ordered Jerry calmly. Unshaken, he continued the flight, while Shirley and the Oakleys wiped cold perspiration from their brows. And there was that sudden downdraft in a driving rain over Omaha—the plane was being relentlessly borne to the earth. Jerry calmly killed the engine letting the plane win its own fight with the forces of gravity. He appeared utterly unaffected; his three passengers confessed later to ''three nervous breakdowns.'' In the air, he didn't make mistakes.

One of his great triumphs in the field of taped material involved his contacts with Henry Ford II, when he convinced the latter that stereo equipment should be produced for the automobile.

''The automobile is a perfect sound chamber,'' Jerry told this famous man. ''There's no better place to listen to music.''

And Henry Ford II agreed.

Through these years, with homes in Glendale and Loma Linda, California, the Pettis family were always faithful in church attendance. And Jerry sat on many denominational boards, gave free advice when asked, and proposed and showed how new programs could be implemented.

But his love for the ''wide open spaces'' was as strong as ever. Where could he find a place in California that was both ''wide open'' and beautiful—and could prove profitable? Around 1953 he found such a place—the Pauma Valley, on the slopes of Mount Palomar, about 25 miles from San Diego. The view from almost any part of the property was breathtaking—one could see clear off to the Pacific Ocean on one side.

''I'm going to buy this property and grow citrus fruits and avoca-

BUSINESSMAN

dos here," he calmly announced one day.

For once, his friends—and Shirley—were struck dumb. Why, the acreage he had shown them consisted of granite boulders too big to move, and rattlesnakes and sagebrush too thick to kill off—so the "experts" said. That was all Jerry needed. The word "It can't be done" shot instant adrenalin through every part of his body and set his imagination to soaring. He consulted agricultural experts. He became an authority himself on the kind of soil needed for the orchards he visioned. He set out to learn all he could about the growing of citrus and avocados.

"After all," he mused to himself, "this valley is so sheltered on all sides that the danger of frost is practically nil. The project can't fail!"

And it didn't. Years of work and expertise went into Rancho del Cielo Grande ("Ranch of the Big Sky"), but today the Pettis citrus and avocado groves seem determined to outproduce anything ever seen or heard of in that line before.

Of course it didn't happen overnight. At first he and Shirley bought a couple of tiny house trailers, which they parked under the trees. No plumbing facilities. (This most fastidious of men could still rough it when necessary.) Immediately Jerry bought some horses and stabled them on the property; the children and Shirley and the Marshes and the Oakleys and dozens of other friends spent delightful weekends on horseback, exploring the mountains. Jerry, though, never came to regard a horse as anything but an animal of work. He loved to groom and saddle the creatures, but he never did much riding. He was too busy planning where he and Shirley would build their house. Just where could they get the best view?

They covered every foot of their property, Shirley says, trying to envision just what a house would be like on this or that spot. Finally they settled on the location. But the more they thought of it, the more unsure they were that this was *the* place. And Jerry always had to be *sure*. Finally, though, they chose the spot, designed a beautiful, rambling, yet homey ranch house, and built.

There were "insurmountable" problems—how to get a water supply. Jerry solved it by damming up some of the streams and installing plastic water pipes. In fact, he designed the route of the water system, right down to the last spigot.

63

Congressman Pettis finds relaxation with Shirley, Pete, and Debbie and their pets at their Pauma Valley Ranch. But farewells (upper right) precede another busy Washington stint.

And the land had to be cleared, and the young trees put in, and the right foreman hired, and—but Jerry—with Shirley's enormous executive ability beside him—proved equal to the challenges.

In the last years of his life, true happiness, true tranquillity, release from tension, bright and shining happiness—this is what Rancho del Cielo Grande represented to him. He treasured every moment he could spend there. He would discard his elegant "congressional" suits, get into old jeans and shirt, and ride his tractor through the groves, inspecting his trees with the loving care of a parent. He mastered the art of successful tree grafting, among other skills.

Shirley ran a veritable hotel for their friends, who now numbered literally in the hundreds—thousands, perhaps. Everyone loved to be "at the ranch."

Claron Oakley sums it up best, perhaps: "Jerry was born out of his time. He would have made a great John C. Fremont; and no better example of his pioneering spirit survives than the present-day Rancho del Cielo Grande in Pauma Valley."

Jerry had been minister, aviator, teacher, public-relations expert, businessman. Financially, he was secure. He had traveled over most of the world.

Now he must have a new challenge. He had always been interested in the theories of government; he had always, from the time when he advocated a "twenty-one-year-old President of the United States," wanted to serve his country and see needed changes effected.

Of course. He would enter politics.

The Congressman / 6

Of course, the decision to run for Congress didn't happen over-night. Jerry never entered into any project without a cool and clear-headed analysis of the possibilities. He consulted with many people in his area on the subject, taking as his prime adviser Dr. Alonzo Baker, well-known political scientist from University of the Pacific and Loma Linda University. Dr. Baker had himself made an unsuc-cessful bid for Congress earlier and felt that his knowledge of what he considered to be mistakes could prove beneficial to Jerry.

Finally it had all been talked out, first and foremost with Shirley, with Dr. and Mrs. McCumber, with the Louis Fishers, the Marshes, the Oakleys, with—but it's impossible to list all the names. One last talk with Dr. Baker. "This is it. Shall I announce my candidacy and file the necessary papers?" Jerry asked.

"The sooner the better!" exclaimed Dr. Baker, himself an intel-lectual and energetic and undefeated personality.

And so it all began—the organizing of the attempt, the campaign managers, the arranging for public appearances, the bringing in of funds, all the welter of details which have become familiar to most Americans in recent years since the lives of congressmen have come under such close scrutiny. Jerry and Shirley gave it all they had.

Jerry *lost* by a little less than 1 percent.

"How in the world could such a thing have happened?" was the question on the lips of all Jerry's friends and admirers, worldwide. Jerry *did not lose*. Jerry *always* won.

Berneva and Louis Fisher commiserated at once. Bob and Mar-guerite Marsh joined the "party." They recalled that one of the cam-paign activities had been a dinner at the Orange Show grounds in San Bernardino. Dr. Edward Annis, president of the American Medical Association, had given a talk full of praise and endorsement for Jerry.

65

Jerry Pettis
LOMA LINDA, CALIFORNIA

November 22, 1966
3:30 AM

Dearest "Torah" —

I don't know what we've gotten ourselves into — but I hope it fits into God's great design.

While I write hundreds of notes to others — thanking them for little favours — I don't want to forget that the better part of this team of Pettis & Pettis is you!

Thank you, Sweetheart, for "going along" with me on this adventure & for working twice as hard at it as I have!

Lovingly —

J

Letter from Jerry to Shirley after their first successful campaign.

Jerry and Shirley pose on Capitol Building steps.

Then Bob and Marguerite had sung a duet. Semiprofessionals that they were, they painfully tried to joke about their singing.

"Do you think our song had anything to do with your defeat?" they teased Jerry.

"Well," Bob reminisces, with a wry smile, "Jerry assured us that it didn't, but I wonder if it is more than coincidence that he never asked us to sing at a political rally again!"

The Marshes felt sufficiently responsible for the defeat (they joked) that they suggested a foursome vacation near Solvang, California, at a dude ranch. Jerry, who had grown up on a horse in Arizona, rode with the other three all day long under the moss-draped trees. This exercise may have been an attempt to dilute his disappointment. In the evenings, the saddle-weary couples played table games and laughed constantly. In Jerry's philosophy, that was better than crying.

Meanwhile, his friends were discussing—as usual—Jerry.

"I wonder how he'll handle this defeat," Kenneth Wood remarked to Charles Anderson. "Do you think he'll give up the whole idea?"

Charles Anderson, now a well-known psychiatrist, answered immediately.

"Not on your life. He'll run again and he'll win."

He did.

And so began the Washington years, the congressional years.

When the final results of the election were known late one night in November of 1966, Jerry turned to Shirley, in the midst of the victory celebration, and whispered, "What have we gotten ourselves into?"

Shirley had reason to remember that question many times in the succeeding two months before they must be in Washington, D.C., for the swearing-in. Their business empire had to be put in competent hands. Their several residences had to be provided with either caretakers or relatives to live in them. But most pressing of all, they had to have a place to live in Washington. Debbie was only eight, and Peter eleven; they were in school; Shirley had been away from them much more than she deemed best, due to the rigors of the campaign. She found herself exhausted, physically and emotionally, from the endless round of luncheons, teas, dinners, rallies—on the well-known "campaign trail."

"Shirley, you'll just have to make a trip back to Washington by yourself and find something at least temporary for us to live in," Jerry told her one night. "My hands are full, trying to get the business and the ranch sorted out."

Used to making decisions, Shirley wasn't terrorized in any way, but somehow she had envisioned that they would make the trip together. "Should have known better," she scolded herself.

"Well, what sort of housing do you visualize?" she wanted to know. Jerry had very definite ideas about the sort of place he enjoyed living in.

"A house," he told her. "Not an apartment."

"How about furniture? We can't dismantle the ranch."

Stricken, he gazed at her. Dismantling his beloved ranch was out of the question.

"I wonder how other congressmen manage?" was his question.

"Any way they can," was Shirley's rather grim rejoinder, as the reality of the nitty-gritty was borne in upon her.

Shirley eventually dismantled the Loma Linda house and shipped that furniture east.

Arriving in cold, gray Washington, D.C. in winter is not exactly an experience guaranteed to lift the spirits of an ardent Californian. Shirley had something along which *did* lift her spirits, however. It was Jerry's "victory gift" to her—a full-length, blond mink coat, so soft and light and warm that not even the bitter winds of the nation's capital could chill either her body or her spirits.

Barely taking time to check into a hotel, she put herself under the counsel of a Virginia realtor who had been recommended to her. Shirley, a born executive, had taken the trouble to assess distances from the Capitol building to various D.C., Maryland, and Virginia areas. She had decided that it was a relatively short drive across Chain Bridge to the Virginia side. She would concentrate on that area.

After several days of looking, her spirits were somewhat dampened in spite of the coat. Buying so soon seemed a financial risk. What if they didn't like the neighborhood? But rental houses were conspicuous by their nonexistence. And a *furnished* rental house? The agent simply smiled at her in a most superior way and kept trying to sell this property and that to her. Finally, though, he realized that this beautiful, gentle woman had a backbone of reinforced concrete.

Early one morning he phoned her in her hotel room.

"Mrs. Pettis, I think I've found it. There's an army officer who's been sent suddenly overseas. He and his wife have a lovely home; they want to rent it to a very responsible person. Can you settle for the house without furniture?"

"Yes—if it's the right house! Can you pick me up in fifteen minutes?"

The Pettis luck was working as usual. The house lived up to all specifications in size and location. Shirley signed a year's lease on the spot, caught the next plane for California, and announced to Jerry, when he met her at the airport, "We're all set!"

Before the exodus to Washington, the Pettises and the Marshes decided to have one last "fling." The two couples, with two children each, rented a fishing boat in San Diego for a day. This was a deep-sea, thirty-five-foot trawler, which came complete with captain and crew. Grandly they proceeded out from the harbor into the swells off-shore from La Jolla. None of them were experienced fishermen, but all had been instructed in the use of the equipment, in baiting the hooks, and landing the fish.

Characteristically, Jerry took over on the boat as an advanced instructor. Alas, when the boat reached its destination, and the captain turned off the motor, the incessant swell brought on cases of violent seasickness for the eight passengers.

Jerry, though as green around the gills as the rest, absolutely refused to admit his mal de mer and resolutely refused to "feed the fish." He was the only one with that record, and to this day Bob Marsh doesn't know how Jerry exerted that much mind over so much matter. But Jerry didn't protest when the other passengers pitifully begged the captain to turn the ship toward shore and make for home as rapidly as possible.

Then came the packing in earnest, the endless decisions as to what to take and what not to take, the decision that Jerry should fly to Washington and stay in a hotel while Shirley prepared the house for the advent of the moving van and drove one of the cars (with the children) east. Even Jerry was surprised that it finally all dovetailed.

"I really like this house," he announced, after the worst of the settling in was over. "Good job, Shirley."

Basking in his admiration, Shirley didn't regret the hours she had spent looking for accessories to make the house seem more their own. She had used, with the white furniture and carpets, splashes of red velvet with cushions. She had bought a red velvet chair and a red bedspread and drapes for their room. Red was a favorite color of Jerry's. He "felt good" with red.

In between the household matters came the incessant meetings for freshmen congressmen and their wives, the indoctrination sessions.

Jerry began to lose weight alarmingly. A man with a rather large frame, he could easily look gaunt and hollow-eyed, which he emphatically did. One of his friends at an evening dinner became solicitous regarding his health.

"Actually," Jerry answered, "I'll have to admit that I've never been so tired in my life. I wonder if the average person realizes what an overwhelming thing it is to become a member of Congress. You don't know one single thing about it when you're first elected. You don't even know how to get your paycheck. You don't know where your committee assignments are. You don't know—well, name it and you don't know it!"

A man with a different temperament doubtless would have taken things as they came and would have put no pressure on himself or any time limits for mastery of an almost impossible job. Not Jerry. That was never his modus operandi. He got up every morning at 5:30, showered, and then went to his office, where he plunged into the day's mail, stopping only to go to the cafeteria for a scanty breakfast. Then the mail, the mail, the mail. They carried it in in gunnysacks. His loyal staff, recruited from both California and Washington, were amazed at his determination to answer every constituent, every request.

"These are the people that sent me here," he told them. "I'm their servant. You know how I feel about government getting so far removed from the people that a citizen with a problem is almost driven mad trying to find help. Well, in my office my constituents are going to *find* that help, and I'm going to solve their problems if I can."

As the years went on, his mail would reach such monumental proportions that even he was staggered. He insisted that files be kept of requests, of the status of pending problems, of unsolved problems, and of unsolvable problems. A favorite question to his personal secretary, Susan Fitts, during his last term was, "Has that been written down?"

Susan, harassed beyond words, might reply, "Yes, in my head."

And he would invariably answer, "What if you got hit by a streetcar?"

This exchange later grew into the legend of "Congressman Pettis's streetcar theory."

Shirley faced great problems of her own there at the beginning. The two children, uprooted from friends, home, and the familiar schools, felt like "strangers in a strange land." They, especially Pete, didn't like the new schools. He longed for what used to be. And his suffering was keenly felt by Shirley.

One night she heard Pete, the most self-contained of boys, go weeping quietly to his bed.

"What's the matter, dear?" she asked, sitting down beside him.

"Oh, Mother, I want to go home!" he burst out, dry sobs racking his slender body. "Do we have to stay here?"

Cut to the heart, she could find no words of real comfort.

"We couldn't let Daddy down, could we?" she whispered.

These were magic words. Pete idolized his father. After a moment, while he struggled to regain his composure, he assured her that he was all right.

But he paid a price—stomach ulcers at the ripe old age of 12.

Debbie, a child of a flexible, sanguine temperament made her adjustment after the first few weeks and continued to sail through the year with literally no problems.

But if the Pettis family had that blessing, they also had some that hid behind a question mark. For instance, there were the problems of constant social life and the securing of household help. A congressman and his wife are invited to several social occasions every night in the week. Naturally, they cannot attend all of them, but some are almost a "must" in protocol-conscious Washington. Jerry quickly learned to keep his tux and evening shoes and clean dress shirt in his private bathroom, so that Shirley could pick him up for whatever dinner, concert, reception, musical, or political meeting they were scheduled to attend. The House session seldom permitted his return home in time to change. If the social occasion wasn't a dinner, many times he had no dinner at all or just a sandwich at his desk.

Shirley was able to secure the services of "baby-sitters"—a term the two children keenly resented, feeling that their age required, rather, "people-sitters" in the evenings. Shirley herself was in perpetual motion, attending the daytime events which Jerry insisted that she must attend. It was vital to get acquainted with Washington. It was absolutely necessary to see and be seen, if he was to become the effective congressman that his personal goal demanded.

Shirley, who had employed household help for years, could not seem to find anything more satisfactory than the services of an occasional day worker. She had already begun, almost as soon as she arrived, to entertain old friends living in the area, and in a few short weeks she and Jerry must begin their formal entertaining.

One night she was driven almost to despair when Jerry arrived home with about fifteen minutes to spare before they must leave for a reception.

"I've decided that the only reason I came back to Washington is to scrub toilets!" Shirley burst out, having just performed that unsavory chore in the three bathrooms of the house, in addition to scrubbing the floors and polishing the faucets.

"I can't stand to think of your doing that sort of thing," Jerry told her. He never liked to see Shirley cleaning or cooking; to him, her role was that of a beautiful and gracious hostess and an informed political partner.

With all the bills before Congress, and committee appointments, Jerry found himself carrying home a briefcase full of work each night which he attacked after the social part of the evening was over. This meant that he was getting only a few hours of sleep each night. It is popular currently to describe congressmen as "goof-offs" who spend their time in rather questionable places, but it is hardly fair to class all in this category. Jerry Pettis emphatically was not. When he cast his vote, whatever the issue, he was determined to know as much as possible about the issue. He knew that his constituents expected this of him.

"Shirley, I can't turn my mind off," he told her late one night—in the early morning, actually. "I just can't stop cerebrating."

She was convulsed. Who but Jerry would use the word "cerebrating"? Most people would settle for "thinking."

Then there were the trips to "the district" in California almost every other weekend, every Congressional recess, and every holiday, with each trip crammed to the hilt with speaking engagements. During the first year, Shirley couldn't go "home" with him, because there was no one to stay with the children. In later years, when the children were older and in boarding schools, she either accompanied him, or went at alternate times, so that they knew constantly the "pulse" of their constituents and their attitudes on the most urgent issues.

"How can you stand that constant flying back and forth to the West Coast?" an old friend asked Jerry.

He looked surprised. "No problem," he declared. "I buy a first-class ticket on my old airline, United, for a night flight, and if there's room, the stewardesses let me stretch out on three seats in the economy section. They give me a blanket and a pillow, and I'm asleep before the plane even leaves the ground. They wake me up when we land. Coming back to Washington, I do the same thing, arriving Monday morning, and go straight to the office, where I keep a change of clothes and a razor, etc."

His California office staff met his plane on the West Coast end, and he was "off and running," deluging them with rapid-fire questions, looking over the schedule they had prepared for him, making memos, and—as he put it—cerebrating all the way. Later, he bought his own small plane which he usually kept at the Tri-City Airport near San Bernardino. This provided him with "instant mobility" and also gave him the freedom of the blue sky, which he loved. As that plane grew older, he bought a new one—the final one.

During the first few months in Washington, Shirley spent hours each day as a "glorified chauffeur"—her description. Snow-covered, icy streets didn't add much joy to the picture; several severe skids bore testimony to her bravery in attacking "hazardous driving conditions." And she still chuckles as she recalls a bleak evening after about three weeks in Washington, when she and Pete attempted to pick Jerry up in front of his office building, about six in the evening, at the height of the rush-hour traffic. Only residents of Washington can possibly understand a problem of this sort. Each time she and Pete would feel that they were about to zero in on the building, they would find themselves on a one-way street—the wrong way, for their purposes.

They drove around and around, until Pete, desperate, burst out, "Mother, let's just get out on the highway and head back to California!"

"Don't tempt me, Pete," she answered, grimly.

After about one and a half years of the rented house, Shirley's strong home-loving nature began to alert her that it was time to put some real roots down in Washington.

"I've been looking for a house to buy," she told Jerry, with elaborate casualness, "and I've found just what you'll like."

He groaned in mock dismay.

"It's going to cost me something, I'm sure of that. What's the price?"

But Shirley refused to tell him.

"Come and look at it first. Then we'll discuss the minor matter of price," she urged.

He did look, and he liked what he saw. The price didn't seem excessive, and they bought a beautiful house in the Spring Valley section of Washington, D.C., only a few minutes' ride from his office. It wasn't purchased without some fear and uneasiness, however; the '68 election hadn't yet taken place. After Shirley had finished decorating and furnishing the lovely home, Jerry seemed much more content, his spirit much more at ease. And he enjoyed his next-door neighbors, George and Barbara Bush. Mr. Bush, who later spent time in China as a United States envoy, still later became director of the C.I.A.

During the first few weeks in Washington, one of the most pleasant evenings Jerry and Shirley spent was at a reception given in Takoma Park, Maryland, where the world headquarters of the Seventh-day Adventist Church is located. Old friends hosted a reception for literally thousands of people in one of the auditoriums of the Sligo Elementary School. It had been hoped that the guest list could be kept down a bit, so that Jerry and Shirley wouldn't have to stand on their feet indefinitely, but as the plans progressed, it became obvious that *everyone* wanted to shake hands with them. And so they stood, gracious and charming, hour after hour, while a string quartet played soft music.

"Isn't she beautiful?" was the comment over and over, coupled with, "Isn't he the most charming man you've ever met?"

Later on, after they had moved to their Spring Valley home, Shirley finally found "live-in" domestic help, which simplified things a great deal. It came in good time, for by now many of their personal friends and valued constituents were their house guests, sometimes for weeks. Shirley remarked that now she really *could* qualify for a chauffeur's license, since she drove fifteen miles across the city each morning to take the children to their Seventh-day Adventist schools, and since she picked up so many people at the three airports in the metropolitan Washington area.

Sabbaths (Saturdays) always found the entire family, when in Washington, attending either the Capital Memorial Seventh-day Adventist Church, just off Connecticut Avenue, near downtown Washington, the 3000-member Sligo Church in Takoma Park, or the Takoma Park Church, the latter two within two miles of each other. The Pettis family worshiped quietly, expecting no special recognition or treatment. Jerry kept close contact with world church leaders, and his office was always open to them; he addressed many official church gatherings, sharing his insights and advising on matters of importance.

Though he never was ambitious to be a "fashion plate," Jerry had a kind of built-in elegance. He wore his clothes very well indeed, and he had decided ideas as to how he wanted to look. His wardrobe consisted almost entirely of black, navy, or gray suits, either plain or with very, very muted patterns. His shirts, custom-made, were nearly always white, or at the most, pale blue, with the embroidered monogram, "JP" on the pocket. Even when garish colors and gaudy ties were the "in" thing, Jerry never succumbed to their lure. He would go as far as turtleneck sweaters and leisure suits, but no purple shirts and ties, thank you!

Pete and Debbie grew up in the midst of all this, hearing names like "Nixon" and "Kissinger" and "Lyndon Johnson" as familiar to them as "Smith" and "Jones." Summers, of course, meant California, and meant that they could have more of their mother, who set aside that time, no matter what. But their father never could spend the time he might have wished with them.

People often wonder how a public personality such as Jerry Pettis can squeeze in time for his children. And the answer is that he never can spend as much as they might wish. This is one of the sacrifices made by men in very demanding professions—senators, congressmen, ministers, etc. But fatherhood may have been more difficult for Jerry than for some other men because he had had such a hard road to success himself. His resolve never to depend on anyone else for anything, and never to ask or give quarter, made at times for an uneasy relationship with his children, who looked upon him as a god of sorts. Perfectionist in everything that he did, he sometimes did not realize that children mature slowly—most children, that is. Jerry himself was born mature.

But as far as he could fit things in, Jerry did not let them down. When Debbie graduated from the eighth grade at John Nevins Andrews School in Takoma Park, all the class badly wanted to have Congressman Pettis as their graduation speaker. But do you ask a United States Congressman to address an eighth grade class? "Of course you do when he's your father," Debbie declared. This request came at a particularly busy time for Jerry, but it would not have occurred to him to refuse. He even took the time to look up some documentation on the scope and growth of the private school system of the Seventh-day Adventist Church. Debbie sat in her own private glow as her handsome, successful, magnetic father gave the occasion just as much attention as he would have given to a gathering of the most elite adults.

As Pete grew into a teen-ager, Jerry had no intention of permitting him to become the typical rich man's son. Pete wanted a car. Very well, he could get a job to earn the money for the payments. He spent long hours working at various semimenial jobs to pay for his very modest little Mustang. But Pete understood his father's reasoning. And it is poignant beyond words to recall that Pete, himself a professional flier at the time of Jerry's death, insisted on accompanying the search party who found the wreckage of the plane. Pete had absorbed some of the iron in his father's soul; he was a tower of strength to Shirley when she most needed his young masculine support and solace.

In describing her father, Debbie says: "The earliest memory I have of my dad dates to when we were still living in Loma Linda in an apartment. Sometimes I used to ride with him to Los Angeles to his office. He was always here and there, getting things done himself. He never depended on anyone else to do his job, and often to make

77

sure things were done right, he'd take over other people's jobs also.

"When I think about him, the word that comes to my mind is *responsibility*. Because that was practically his whole being. He loved a challenge and he stuck to it. His ideas and inventiveness were extraordinary. He stressed responsibility to us kids and would come down on us if we slipped.

"I think his strongest influence in my life was his philosophy of going past the limit most people go. He stressed that all the time. Take my brother, for instance. My father felt that if Pete was to go into flying, he should go *all* the way. Do better than an average flier. And that's had a big impact on all the ideas of my brother and me. He wanted us to have every possible training we would need.

"As a disciplinarian, he could scare the daylights out of anyone! And on several occasions he did. I've known few instances when he actually spanked us, but he was *very* effective with his voice. And he was sometimes stubborn. He would hear *no* backtalk, even if perchance we were right and could show him the evidence, he still wouldn't budge. That got to be extremely hard to cope with during my early teen years.

"We always realized that he had high goals for us—plenty of education, and settle for nothing but the best. He allowed a certain freedom of expanding ideas, but on several issues he was just as conservative as a 90-year-old! I think the main thing is that he let us choose what we were interested in, and then he pushed us along through it. He didn't make us feel superior, but he stressed that if you work for something, like he did, you deserved to get what you wanted. He did *not* like overexcessive dreams.

"He handled things as he progressed up the ladder. He was the 'Start from the bottom, because if you don't, you'll never make it' kind of person. He used his own life as an example in talking to us. But he didn't discuss anything about philosophies of living. Maybe that was because we understood it without its being said. Just take one look at his life, and that's as much philosophy as you could stuff into thirty people!

"As far as I am concerned, his most beautiful accomplishment in life was apart from all his titles; it was his love for the people in his district and the love he got in return.

"The big disappointment of my life is that I saw so little of him.

He was always out in the district, seeing his people. There wasn't much time to exchange thoughts or do things together.

"If I were describing him to someone who knew nothing about him, these are the words I would use, consideration, love of challenge, compassion to those in need, love of life and all that's in it.

"He loved to see us kids laugh at his jokes. He didn't laugh a lot himself, but he liked to see people happy.

"I can remember only one specific time he actully came out and said, 'I love you' in the closest words he could find. 'How proud I am of the way you are maturing. Your cheerfulness, your accomplishments in school, make me *very* happy.' This was in a letter he wrote me on November 17, 1974.

"This is the only time I ever got such praise, because my dad didn't believe in praise until you did the job the best you could, and often he felt that it wasn't the best. Thus, any praise from him meant more to both Pete and me.

"I truly believe that his life will go on as an inspiration for generations to come."

And so the years passed like lightning for Congressman Jerry Pettis, his wife, and his children. They crowded about forty-eight hours of living into each twenty-four-hour period. Their trips over the world on congressional business were sandwiched in with the sessions of the House and the constant trips to the thirty-seventh District of California. For instance, there was the incredible trip to China, when they were part of a congressional delegation, and guests of the Chinese government. Richard Nixon was President at the time. Their Air Force plane stopped at San Clemente for a final briefing.

"Don't forget," Mrs. Nixon told the women, "that you are representing the United States government."

Seeing China, where he had flown transport planes during the war, was a dreamlike experience for Jerry. He shared his observations and conclusions, as well as his pictures, with many groups upon his return.

The two of them—Jerry and Shirley—forged an ever-closer partnership, an ever-deeper understanding. They knew they could *count* on each other. Shirley wondered if Jerry was carrying it a bit too far, however, at a banquet where Jerry was scheduled as the speaker.

He had been unusually quiet during the meal. She realized that he

Pettis's natural courtesy and sincerity gain Premier Chou En Lai as a friend.

A group of small children in a school in China give their welcome to Congressman Pettis in smiles and handshakes.

was tired to the point of exhaustion. He said nothing indicative of this, however, and, when he was introduced, arose with his usual gracious manner, greeted the guests, told them that he was delighted to see them, and then turned to Shirley, with his irresistible charm, and announced, "I have a surprise for you. Shirley is going to be the speaker tonight. She's just had a personal tour of the family quarters of the White House by Mrs. Lyndon Johnson, and I know she'd *love* to tell you about it!"

Taken 100 percent by surprise, Shirley struggled to her feet, amid enthusiastic applause. "I could cheerfully have wrung his neck," she said later. "I had no idea that I'd be saying a word."

She gave a fantastically good speech according to an expert— Jerry. When she chided him in their hotel room later, rather heatedly, he only smiled benignly, "I knew you could do it," he told her. "And I was so tired I thought I wouldn't make sense."

After Gerald Ford became vice-president, Jerry and Shirley attended a social event at one of the elegant Washington hotels where, after dinner, the women were taken into one of the smaller rooms and the men into another. It turned out that the ladies were to be entertained by a singer. Shirley settled down to enjoy herself. After about fifteen minutes, she noticed a handsome young man approaching her at a half-crouch, so that he wouldn't disrupt the program. As he reached her side, he knelt down and whispered, "The vice-president is leaving now. Do you wish to go home with him?"

Instantly Shirley grasped what had happened. Her resemblance to Betty Ford had been commented on by others during the past few weeks. This was Betty's secret service man, taking care of what he thought was the vice-president's wife.

Without cracking a smile, she whispered back, "I'd love to, but I don't think Mrs. Ford would like it."

The young secret service man blushed to the roots of his hair and made a hasty exit.

Jerry laughed about it with Shirley, but then he grew thoughtful.

"I think you better change your hair style, Shirley," he told her. "I want you to be recognized as Mrs. *Pettis*, not Mrs. *Ford*."

Shirley basked in his possessiveness.

Shirley will one day write her own book about the Washington days when Jerry was a Congressman and they were a team. It is a cherished ambition of hers. But that must come later, when the past is not so close to the present, and when her rememberings are not so colored with sadness.

Finally, it was February 1975. Congress would be in recess. The two of them would return to California to a round of political engagements. On the night of February 13, they would stay at the Palm Springs Tennis Club, they would attend a dinner, would get to bed very late, would have to get up very early in the morning to meet separate appointments.

Their plane was in Palm Springs at the airport, for Jerry planned to fly back to Tri-City Airport in San Bernardino, while Shirley drove the car into Glendale for a day with Berneva Fisher. As they drove together to the Palm Springs airport, Shirley was disturbed because Jerry looked so worn, so exhausted.

"Jerry, why don't you leave the plane here and drive with me as far as San Bernardino?" she suggested. "You can have about an hour's sleep that way."

He thought for a moment.

"I really don't have the time. The press conference has been set up with the idea that I'd be flying. I don't like to keep all those people waiting. And this is Friday—I'll get a good rest tonight."

When they pulled up at the airport, he kissed her good-bye, and got out of the car.

"See you tonight, Love," he told her.

Congressman Pettis prepares to speak in Congressional Committee Room.

At Gettysburg with the late Dwight Eisenhower and Gerald Ford.

Opposite page: Gerald Ford, minority leader in 1964, campaigns with Jerry and Shirley and Debbie in San Bernardino in Jerry's first Congressional venture.

For CONGRESSMAN
PETTIS
ELECT
PETTIS
CONGRESSMAN
ELECT
PETTIS
CONGRESSMAN

Opposite, upper left: With Secretary of the Treasury John Connally, 1971, when Connally testified before the House Ways and Means Committee.

Opposite, upper right: With Secretary of State William Rogers, 1970.

Opposite, lower: With Secretary of the Treasury William Simon, 1974.

At the George C. Marshall Space Flight Center in Huntsville, Alabama, in 1967, Congressman Pettis discusses space technology with Wernher von Braun.

Pettis is awarded the "Invest in America Eagle Award" in 1970.

DEL ANKERS PHOTO

A typical day's mail in the Congressman's office.

Overleaf: At White House breakfast, 1970, with Congressmen
Schwenzel (Iowa), Miller (Ohio), and Winn (Kansas) in foreground.

WHITE HOUSE PHOTO

Presenting to Gerald Ford his picture painted by Artist George Akimoto of California.

Opposite, upper: Pettis speaks to the Ways and Means Committee of which he later became ranking member.

Opposite, lower: Jerry testifies at the fire hearings in 1973.

EL ANKERS PHOTO

Mrs. Shirley Pettis carries on the work begun by her esteemed husband and is elected to Congress in her own landslide victory.

Congressional Record of Jerry L. Pettis

Jerry L. Pettis, late representative from California's thirty-seventh district, was first elected to the House of Representatives in 1966. He was a member of the powerful Ways and Means Committee at the time of his death—and had the distinction of being the second man in this century to gain this post after only three years of congressional service. Ways and Means writes the laws on all personal and corporate taxes, Social Security and related health-care programs, trade and tariff regulations and other vital areas.

After joining the committee, Congressman Pettis helped author comprehensive welfare reforms, the penalties portion of the Drug Control and Rehabilitation Act, Social Security increases totaling 15 percent, middle-income oriented tax reforms, airport and airways funding regulations, new trade agreements, and a revenue-sharing plan designed to help states and localities.

Jerry also served on the special Congressional Task Force on National Health and was a member of the Earth Resources and Population Task Force. He was an advisor to the National Commission on Fire Prevention and Control and a former member of the Congressional Policy Committee.

As an acknowledged expert in the health-care field, Congressman Pettis was in great demand as a speaker advocating new approaches to improve the national health-care delivery system. His interest and background also led to his recognized role as a strong advocate of improved educational programs.

Christian Science Monitor *honored him in its choice of Outstanding Congressmen. He received the Watchdog of the Treasury award for support of thrift in government spending, achieved a 100 percent national security index rating, and was given numerous commendations for service and leadership in the Congress.*

He served on the House Science and Astronautics Committee from 1966 to 70; the House Administration Committee, 1966 to 1968; and the House Ways and Means Committee, 1970 to 1975.

Other than the various committee bills, the most important of which was the Trade Reform Act of 1974, Jerry Pettis's major legislative efforts focused on enactment of his California Desert Protection Bill, which he introduced in three Congresses. The measure was not passed by the House during his life, but was included in the so-called Bureau of Land Management Organic Act.

His foreign travels on official government business include the following:

1967. November 3 to 13. Member of U.S. official delegation to dedication of astronomical observatory at Cerro Tololo, Chile. Delegation also went to Peru, Brazil, Bahamas, Venezuela.

1968. January. Member of congressional fact-finding delegation to inspect U.S. military facilities in Vietnam and other Southeast Asia countries. Visited Antarctica as well.

December 1969 to January 1970. Member of House Science and Astronautics Committee delegation to inspect facilities and research projects in Antarctica.

1972. January 5 to 13. Part of House Ways and Means Committee delegation to France and Belgium for meetings with European Economic Community (Common Market) officials.

1973. July 1 to 20. Member of Congressional delegation to the People's Republic of China.

1974. May 26 to June 2. Delegate from House Ways and Means Committee at meeting of Organization of Economic Cooperation and Development.

"Because I could not stop for death,
he kindly stopped for me."

—Emily Dickinson

The Last Homecoming / 7

The flag-draped, bronze coffin sat in silent majesty at the front of the church, flanked on either side by three strong, handsome, polished members of the Air Force Honor Guard from nearby Norton Air Force Base, so motionless in their position that they seemed like young statues.

He was home. Jerry was on the campus of Loma Linda University, the school so dear to him, and with which he had been associated for more than nineteen years. He was in the church that he had always regarded as his home church, despite the many others he had attended on Sabbaths in his travels over the world. This was where he belonged, among his people.

Shirley had tried to comfort herself with this thought—that this would be what he would have chosen—all through the anguished, sleepless hours of Monday night. Refusing to take any but the most minimal of medication ("My mind must be clear for all the decisions I have to make"), she had survived—somehow. The planning; the arranging. The ceaseless telephoning back and forth among the California offices and to the Washington office. The notifying of all the California delegation, and the Ways and Means Committee. The funeral arrangements. It went on and on, endlessly.

The death of a great man is not a simple thing.

But in the midst of it all, oases of love and support. First, her children. When Debbie, at her private school in La Jolla, was notified, she phoned her mother immediately at the Loma Linda residence of her grandparents, the McCumbers, knowing instinctively that this was where Shirley would be, comforting them.

"Mother," said this strong sixteen-year-old, "shall I meet you at the ranch or at Loma Linda?"

From then on, she never left her mother's side, but her weeping was done in private. To Shirley, she was support and solace and the promise that the future still held something to live for.

THE LAST HOMECOMING

Pete, a professional flier at 19, had insisted on being with the search parties until the plane was found. His father's philosophy of courage had taken root in the tall, blond, handsome boy. "I have to see for myself; I can't spend the rest of my life wondering," he had told those who had tried to dissuade him, setting his jaw in the characteristic "Pettis" way.

And friends—all the outpouring of love and concern which Jerry and Shirley had shown through the years came back in almost a tidal wave. (Dr.) Louis and Berneva Fisher, in Glendale, dropped everything (not a simple arrangement for a busy physician) and met Shirley in Loma Linda. They would stay by her side every moment until after the funeral. And the Marshes. And (Dr.) Joan Coggin. And— But the list was endless.

Shirley had decided that she and the children must go to the seclusion of the ranch immediately. They must have whatever quiet time they could winnow out, time to contemplate, to be together as a family unit, somehow to find acceptance of a fact that could not ever really be accepted. Also, Shirley was concerned about her parents who were no longer young, and not as well as she could hope. They must not be in the center of the storm. Later she would say to a friend characteristically, "I couldn't believe that I was putting my dear, dear mother and father through this agony for the second time." (The friend will never forget the selflessness of that remark.)

Jerry's office staffs, in the California offices and the Washington office, put aside all thought of sleep or rest. He was more than an employer; he was more than a congressman; he was, simply, a man they loved. Everything must be *right* for his final good-bye. Money does not buy this kind of loyalty and supportiveness; it is purchased by respect for character and sincerity.

Somehow Shirley's anguish had been deepened by the fact that Jerry died on Valentine Day, the day of love and romance and delight. Would the time ever come when she would not be reminded by Valentine Day of her sudden premonition? of turning off the freeway? of finding a telephone booth? of having called the Tri-City Airport and having heard those words, like stones dropping on her heart, "No, Congressman Pettis has not arrived here yet"? Would she always remember on Valentine Day the long drive, all alone, to the airport, her pounding heart, and then the waiting, waiting—and then the knowing—and then being driven to her parents' home in Loma Linda—would it always be with her?

Even on the drive to the ranch, she couldn't bear to glance into store windows, filled with—blood-red hearts. "Will I always feel this unbearable horror on Valentine Day?" she questioned herself silently.

An added harassment—and grief does not insulate one from harassment—was the fact that this was a holiday weekend. How, she wondered, could the staff notify all the members of Congress? Of course the story would be carried on television and radio—already it was being broadcast far and wide in California, on that Friday afternoon and evening, but how could everyone who might want to come from Washington be reached?

Then her strong religious faith took over. "This is not for me to worry about," she told herself. "God knows all these things. He knows what is best. Those who need to be reached will be reached. Arrangements will be made."

And they were made. The funeral would be held at one p.m. on Tuesday, February 18. An Air Force plane would bring, as it turned out, many members of Congress.* They would land about two hours before the funeral at nearby Norton Air Force Base.

Shirley knew what she must do, what Jerry would expect of her.

She asked Debbie and Peter to sit down.

"This will be hard for you, I know," she told them, her face white but completely composed. "But we will have many friends flying all the way from Washington just for the funeral. They will fly back immediately afterward. And it is unthinkable that we should not receive them and speak to each one personally. Anything else would be letting Daddy down. We can't do that. We want to know that he would have been proud of us."

The two of them swallowed hard. Receive guests at such a time? Then they rallied. "Of course, Mother," they told her. She knew she could count on them, as they smiled at her, though their eyes were just a little more moist than they would have wished.

And so, in the Fellowship Hall of Loma Linda University Church, this indomitable wife of an indomitable man, with her children beside her, greeted each congressional guest personally. The delegation had been escorted to the church by special police as an

100

honor to Jerry. She thanked them for coming. Others helped in the receiving line, including Elder Neal Wilson, president of the North American Division of the Seventh-day Adventist Church, and another close, loved friend of Jerry's.

At only one point had Shirley suddenly felt that perhaps she could not, after all, manage. Clothes were the last thing she wanted to think about—then suddenly—"What will I wear to the funeral?" she cried, as she and Berneva Fisher were working over the arrangements. "I don't have a black dress, not even one, here in California. It's Sunday afternoon now, and there's so much to do, and I don't believe I could *ever* go into a store tomorrow and buy a dress."

In near despair she laid her head on the table in front of her.

"Shirley, I have a new black dress that I know will be just right for you. We are so near the same size. I'll send to Glendale for it right now. So that's settled," Berneva told her lovingly. And it was. The dress, when it arrived, fitted perfectly.

"I somehow feel that I need just a little more privacy than with an ordinary veil," Shirley remarked wistfully. "I would feel more— protected—if I could have a mourning veil similar to the one Jacqueline Kennedy wore—" she broke off, musing.

Her executive ability was in full command again.

"When hats were the thing, I used to buy most of mine from a certain shop in La Mesa," she told Berneva. "If I can just get the home number of the owner, I feel certain he would have one of his people make me what I need. He is a loyal constituent of Jerry's."

Just how all these miracles were accomplished is unimportant, but they *were* accomplished, and now it was Tuesday, and the reception was over and the funeral must be faced.

At midmorning the crowds had started filing silently into the church, so that by 12:30 every seat was taken. Then a 300-seat chapel annex was opened, and it filled immediately. Even so, hundreds stood about on the outside of the church, listening to the service through loudspeakers which had been installed. More than 3000 people came. It took about thirty sheriffs' deputies to handle the traffic in the tiny university town, which had never seen such an occasion before, and probably never will again. Jerry's people wanted to be near him as long as they possibly could, and so they came from all over the thirty-seventh district, though many had to turn back simply because not one more car could be absorbed into the area. But the service was broadcast in both English and Spanish over the local radio stations.

Shirley had made the firm request, publicly, via the news media, that the service be kept simple. "Jerry would not want this church packed to the ceiling with flowers," she said. She had suggested that those who wished to do so might contribute funds for a chapel in the new veterans' hospital under construction in Loma Linda, to be called the "Jerry L. Pettis Memorial Chapel." (The hospital was being built at this place largely as the result of Jerry's efforts; Congress would later vote that the hospital itself be called "The Jerry L. Pettis Veterans' Memorial Hospital.")

And so there were only about a dozen floral arrangements.

Exactly at 12 noon the Honor Guard had entered and taken their places.

At 12:55 Shirley, her natural radiance eclipsed behind the black dress, the mourning veil, and the dignity of her arrow-straight, tall carriage, entered the church on the arm of Pete, with Debbie and Yvonne (Jerry's daughter by his first marriage; Shirley had arranged at once for her to fly from Northern California) beside her. Shirley knew that the wife of a public servant must be prepared to be photographed even in the midst of the unendurable; she was prepared for the TV cameras that blocked her path momentarily, and she waited with quiet dignity until she could proceed again. Then there were her parents and Jerry's brothers—his mother was not well enough to make the journey.

Their faces grief-stricken, the members of Congress filed down the aisle, two by two, some wives in attendance also, and other famous persons, military, political, social.

Shirley's whole body cried silently, "No!" as the participants filed onto the platform and took their places. But her face remained still, impassive.

As from a great distance, she heard the Loma Linda Brass Ensemble playing "Faith of Our Fathers," and some of the words ran through her mind: "Faith of our fathers living still, in spite of dungeon, fire and sword."

But how could she endure the poignancy of the next item, the most beloved hymn in the world, "The Old Rugged Cross," sung by the King's Heralds, the quartet which has always been a part of "The Voice of Prophecy" radio program? Jerry sometimes substituted in that quartet, she thought to herself, before we met. And he loved that old song.

"I will cling to the old rugged cross, and exchange it someday for a crown."

The words died away.

Shirley felt Pete's rigid young body beside her, his face graven in stone. She knew the inner sensitivity of his nature. Her heart bled for him.

Associate Pastor James Mershon offered a beautiful invocation. "What strength prayer brings," Shirley told herself. "And it is what will comfort me most during the days ahead."

She had wanted Dr. "Bill" Loveless to give the Scripture reading, for Jerry had greatly admired this man's intellectual gifts and sparkling personality. Bill was *his* pastor. But she had never thought to see him standing behind a podium covered with red roses, reading for his fallen friend, those majestic words: "Happy is the man who does not take the wicked for his guide, nor walk the road that sinners tread nor take his seat among the scornful; the law of the Lord is his delight."

Yes, she thought, God's law *was* the delight of Jerry's life, his yardstick.

But Bill was concluding with such comforting texts: "I saw the holy city, new Jerusalem, coming down out of heaven from God, made ready like a bride. . . . He will wipe away every tear from their eyes; there shall be an end to death and to mourning."

Shirley prayed silently: "Please, God, let that day be soon."

Marilyn Cotton, religious radio and television soprano, filled the church with her silvery voice. Jerry and Shirley had spent so many quiet Friday evenings listening to tapes of Marilyn's recordings; more than that, she was a personal friend.

Then it was time for John Rhodes, minority leader of the House of Representatives, to give the congressional eulogy. He read a telegram from President Gerald Ford:

"Betty and I were shocked by the news of Jerry's tragic death, and we send our deepest sympathy to you and your family. Words have so little meaning, but we want you to know you are in our thoughts at this time. Jerry was a dear friend and great American, as well as a devoted husband and father. We hope that the memory of his life will comfort you and that you may find consolation in knowing that Jerry's lifelong commitment to our nation will long be remembered by the people he served so well. His legacy of public service will be a tribute to his memory. We'll be praying for you and your family in the difficult days ahead. Gerald R. Ford.''

Shirley had read that telegram over and over, remembering the many happy times with ''Jerry and Betty'' and ''Jerry and Shirley'' at dinners and other occasions in Washington when they were all ''in the House.'' Then Betty's ''Jerry'' had become vice-president and then President; but they were the same people.

President Ford had also ordered the flag lowered over the White House in loving memory of his friend. Shirley was touched; Jerry would have been embarrassed.

Among other things, Congressman Rhodes declared: ''Congress feels a deep sense of loss at the death of our valued and trusted friend. I never heard anyone say anything bad about Jerry Pettis. We can all take comfort in the fact that we were privileged to know him.''*

He read a telegram from the famous evangelist Billy Graham, who had heard the news while he was in Mexico; and from George and Barbara Bush in Peking, China, where George Bush was U.S. envoy to the People's Republic of China.

''Dear George and Barb,'' thought Shirley. ''Our next-door neighbors in Washington. Almost like family members.''

As she sat there, her mind whirling with the immensity of the dark event, with the solemnity of the service wrapping her in its own special insulation, Shirley thought of Jerry's watch, the one personal item which had been recognizable at the site of the crash. Once, soon after they were married, he had told her that as a small boy he sometimes caddied at one of the elite golf courses in Phoenix.

''I didn't know that there were any watches but the dime-store kind,'' he had said. ''But one day the wealthy man I caddied for showed me a beautiful gold watch. He said, 'Son, this is the Cadillac of all watches, it's a Patek Philippe.'''

---

*See appendix for complete text of remarks and messages.

Jerry's voice had been wistful. "Right there, on that hot golf course, with the perspiration soaking me, I made up my mind that some day I would own a Patek Philippe."

Shirley winced as her thoughts carried her to the small, thin boy.

She too resolved that he would have the watch of his dreams. But somehow they never got around to buying it. Jerry never pampered himself, seldom bought things for his exclusive use.

On his fiftieth birthday, though, Shirley had planned carefully in advance. The Patek Philippe watch, gold and shining, she had purchased—and she had presented it to a suddenly choked-up and overwhelmed Jerry. He always wore it. Now the watch was broken, but was still recognizable, the poignant inscription still readable: "To Jerry, with love long-lasting as the watch. S."

Later, Louis Fisher would send the watch to a famous Swiss jeweler for repairs, adding only, at Shirley's request, the date and minute of Jerry's death, the minute the watch had stopped, upon impact with the mountainside—2-14-75, 8:41. Shirley would wear it on a chain around her neck, the dents which the jeweler could not remove still visible, like the scar on her heart.

Time was passing too swiftly, thought Shirley, almost in panic. All the thousands of people, the casket, the flag, the honor guard, the members of Congress, the service itself—it would soon be over and then—emptiness.

But the King's Heralds were singing again, this time another old and loved and simple hymn, "Nearer, My God, to Thee," and it was time for Dr. Alonzo Baker's tribute.

As this amazing man—now in his eighties, yet seemingly as vigorous as ever, professor of political science, world traveler, one of Jerry's staunchest political mentors and lifelong member of the Seventh-day Adventist Church—spoke of his love for Jerry, his voice broke more than once.

"If the death of Jerry Pettis constitutes an irreparable loss to California and the nation, his loss is an even greater blow to Seventh-day Adventism. Jerry was the first of our faith ever to sit in America's national legislature."*

---

*See appendix for complete text of Dr. Baker's remarks, contained in *Congressional Record* section.

From the moment she knew that Jerry was dead, Shirley had known that there was only one man who must preach his funeral sermon—Dr. H. M. S. Richards, speaker and originator of "The Voice of Prophecy." But would she be able to endure it? Dr. Richards had married them on March 2, 1947—in less than a month they would have celebrated their twenty-eighth anniversary. But no one could comfort her heart as could this gentle, wise, committed Christian man, world famous himself, yet one who had never "lost the common touch."

And he did comfort her. With the resonant voice and deep sincerity that characterize his sermons, Dr. Richards brought peace and a feeling of acceptance to all who listened. His own rocklike faith in God showed through every word. It was obvious that he himself knew whom he had believed.

He spoke of his friendship with Jerry, comparing it to the biblical friendship of David and Jonathan. "O, Jonathan, thou wast slain in thine high places. I am distressed for thee, my brother Jonathan."

"Jesus predicted His own death and resurrection. . . . And when Jesus came forth from Joseph's new tomb, His victory changed the world. And He said, 'Because I live ye shall live also.' His resurrection is a guarantee, the evidence, the proof, that those who believe in Him will live again. . . . Death always comes unexpectedly, really. The summons comes. But we are in the hands of a God who is too wise to make a mistake and too good to be unkind. And that's hard to believe sometimes; it's hard to believe this time. . . . All things are not good, but in God's hands He makes them work together for good to them that love Him; to those who are 'called according to his purpose.'. . .

"Jerry Pettis believed that the whole world is approaching a great crisis, and I am sure that anyone who reads widely today or that travels very much will agree with him. Wonderful things and terrible things are before us, according to Bible prophecy, which Jerry loved. . . . The day will come, as the Scripture says, when they shall 'follow the Lamb whithersoever he goeth' from constellation to constellation, from world to world, with a glad message that the universe is clean. No more sin, no more sorrow, no more deaths, no more rebellion, an endless universe to explore, the vastness of the wisdom of God and of holy beings to begin to understand—that's the

Bible story, and that's what Jerry believed in."*

Shirley was summoning every ounce of her composure and fortitude. For now Dr. Richards had sat down. Now Dr. Loveless was offering a final brief prayer.

Then, almost too much to be borne, a long drum roll, and then, the organ and the brass ensemble.

The next day, in *The Sun-Telegram*, Jan Cleveland and Steve Cooper would say, in reporting the funeral: "A long drum roll marked the beginning of the last hymn, 'The Battle Hymn of the Republic.' Between verses, only the steady drumbeat, punctuated by the sound of quiet sobbing from the audience, could be heard in the church.

"Then the color guard, pallbearers (Philip Rupps, M.D., Louis Fisher, M.D., Harold Ziprick, M.D., Tom Warner, Clinton Emmerson, D.D.S., Robert Marsh, M.D., Robert McLennan, M.D., and Elder Neal Wilson) and casket filed up the main aisle of the church, followed by the family members, stoically attempting to hide their sorrow.

"At the cemetery, the late Congressman was accorded full military honors. Taps were sounded, marksmen fired a three-volley salute, and the color guard ceremoniously presented Mrs. Pettis with the flag from her husband's casket."

Shirley had requested that only the congressional delegation and a few other close friends accompany her and the family to Montecito Memorial Park in nearby Colton. The last part would be the hardest.

It was. When the mournful "taps" sounded across the beautiful San Bernardino Valley, when the flag was placed in her numb hands, she almost broke. But not quite.

Quickly she and the children entered the dark-blue limousine and drove away.

It would not be until two days later that Shirley, on a solitary sunset walk through the citrus groves at "the ranch," would take the green leaves of one of his much loved trees in her hands, bow her head, and let the bitter tears come.

Jerry was gone.

---

*See appendix for full text of Dr. Richards's sermon.

On the Death of a Loved One
Chester A. Holt

Rest, quiet heart. This is the appointed place
Where all the children of our fated race
Foregather; all are leveled at this door.
The poor want nothing here, the rich not more.
You are pavilioned now with queens and kings
And the proud claimants of all earthly things;
And here, except God stay it, we who weep
Shall join you shortly in your quiet sleep.

But not for long will earth's lament be made.
The laggard moments of Time's spent parade—
Like soldiers from lost battles, still in flight—
Press harried movement through the sullen night.
And hard upon them comes God's shining hour
Of resurrection, ecstasy, and power.

Full soon the cadence of triumphant feet
Will throb through space, and 'long the vasty street
Of worlds, God's festive mansions of the sky
Will fling out banners as His hosts pass by.
So to the Father's house the blest will sweep
Where none will die, and none, at last, will weep.

By faith we know, and knowing, can be strong.
Rest, quiet heart, you cannot slumber long.

—*Review and Herald,* June 22, 1972

(Used by permission)

POSTLUDE

"Once the spirit invades the heart, there can be no rest. Even in the dark of night, there is one link in the chain that always holds, one light that will not go out."

—Thomas Wolfe.

———————

And the light did not go out. In a landslide victory, on April 29, 1975, Shirley was elected to Congress, dedicated to carrying on the goals and objectives which were so dear to Jerry.

Appendix

"O God, our help in ages past, our hope for years to come, our shelter from the stormy blast, and our eternal home! Under the shadow of Thy throne, still may we dwell secure; sufficient is Thine arm alone, and our defense is sure. Before the hills in order stood, or earth received her frame, from everlasting Thou art God, to endless years the same. O God, our help in ages past, our hope for years to come; be Thou our guide while life shall last, and our eternal home!"

The death of Jerry Pettis is a great personal loss to me. I'm confident without him there would be no "Voice of Prophecy" today. He encouraged me and helped me. He was our announcer on our coast-to-coast broadcasts, he sang in a quartet and also sang solos, and what he did privately in encouragement to me would take me hours to tell. The first time I ever went up in a plane was because he urged me and almost forced me to go. I never could have carried on my work without the airplane. God bless his memory.

Our text is from Second Samuel, the first chapter. David and Jonathan were great friends—heart friends. The great battle of Gilboa had been fought, and David had just heard the news that Jonathan had died with his father, bravely resisting the advance of the Philistines. "How are the mighty fallen, in the midst of the battle! O Jonathan, thou wast slain in thine high places. I am distressed for thee, my brother Jonathan."

Jerry loved the high places in the sky. And he died there. And when he fell, he leaned upon the breast of a mighty mountain. It was like him. His hope was in the very things that we read in this great Book. He was a simple Christian believer. And Jesus said, you remember, that "he that heareth my word, and believeth on him that sent me, hath [present tense] everlasting life, and shall not come into condemnation; but *is* passed from death unto life." Jerry rests in that hope. He received the words of Christ. He believed in the heavenly Father who sent the Saviour to the world, and therefore he has eternal life and "shall not come into condemnation; but is passed from death unto life."

The Lord Jesus Christ was the Prince of life. Until He came, the world never really knew what life was. All the great ethnic religions had failed to comfort the heart of man. When Jesus came, He changed it all. Every funeral He ever met He broke up by raising the dead. He introduced eternal life to this world and made clear that when He returns in glory all His saints will be immortalized in a world made new—no sickness, no old age, no death, yet as real and actual as this world. All promised, all coming, the signs all fulfilled. The God who was our help in ages past will be our hope in years to come, "a shelter from the stormy blasts and our eternal home."

Jesus said when He heard of the death of Lazarus, His special friend, "I go, that I may awaken him out of sleep." And when He came near the little town of Bethany, (it's about a mile and a half from the east wall of Jerusalem, up on the east side of the Mount of Olives), He sat down and sent word that He was there. Martha, the sister of Lazarus, came as quickly as she could, and her first words were—she had been repeating them over and over all those four days—"If You had been here, he wouldn't have died." And that's the truth!

Jesus said, "Your brother shall live again." We read about this in the eleventh chapter of St. John's Gospel.

And she said, "I know he shall rise again in the resurrection of the last day." And then Jesus said those words we must never forget: "I am the resurrection, and the life: he that believeth in me, though he were dead, yet shall he live: and whosoever liveth and believeth in me shall never die."

Then He went on to the tomb, and at His command the man who had been dead four days came forth, bound hand and foot, as it was the Jews' custom in those days to wrap their dead with hundreds of yards of linen. He came out with the power of God—he didn't walk out. And Jesus said, "Loose him, untie him, let him go. He is a live man."

Jesus had stopped earlier in His ministry, you remember, the cortege with the widow's son, carrying him out to burial. He stopped that funeral and gave the boy back to his widowed mother. And then Jesus predicted His own death and resurrection. He's the only Man who has ever lived who could not only predict the day of His death and the day of His resurrection, but fulfill the prediction. And when Jesus came forth from Joseph's new tomb, it changed the world. And He said, "Because I live, ye shall live also." His resurrection is a guarantee, the evidence, the proof, that those who believe in Him will live again. He said concerning His life, "I have power to lay it down, and I have power to take it again."

"Never man spake like this man," said the officers who came back without the prisoner to the Sanhedrin officers; "we never heard such words." And Jesus made it clear that this life is just a kindergarten to the great university of the hereafter. This is just a beginning; this is a place of test. What we begin here we will finish somewhere else.

Death always comes unexpectedly, really. The summons comes. But we are in the hands of a God who is too wise to make a mistake and too good to be unkind. That's hard to believe sometimes; it's hard to believe this time. The great apostle Paul said, "All things work together for good." If

112

that word "ALL" was not in there, it would be easier for me to believe. But I believe it, by the help of God—"*All* things work together for good." All things are not good, but in God's hands He makes them "work together for good to them that love God, to them who are the called according to his purpose."

Jerry Pettis believed that the whole world was approaching a great crisis, and I am sure that anyone who reads widely today or that travels very much will agree with him. Some great crisis is coming. It's not just in America; it is in the world. The world has never been before as it is now. Wonderful things and terrible things are before us, according to Bible prophecy, which Jerry loved. He knew these great prophecies. He knew that anyone who really believes them must be an optimist in spite of the hard times and sorrows before us. The world's greatest days are just ahead. Times of wonder, blessings, glory, light—man has never really lived yet in this world. When Eden is restored, that image of God which today seems to be almost effaced is to be fully restored in the sons of men.

Why do men risk the skies, why do they want to ascend, why do they want to go in capsules to other planets? They want to be like their Father. God made the world through Jesus Christ. He was the Father in creation, and He made man in His own image. That divine image is not yet effaced in man. He wants to go to the universe; he wants to see for himself; he wants to do; he wants to create. That's the way it should be.

The day will come when, as the Scripture says, "They . . . [shall] follow the Lamb whithersoever he goeth," from constellation to constellation, from world to world, with a glad message that the universe is clean. No more sin, no more sorrows, no more deaths, no more rebellion—an endless universe to explore, the vastness of the wisdom of God and of holy beings to begin to understand. In that great heavenly universe, which will be the university of the future—talk about hope, talk about optimism, talk about wonders! That's the Bible story, and that's what Jerry believed in. He had that gleam in his heart.

He looked forward to that time, spoken of in the last chapter of the Bible, when "God shall wipe away all tears from their eyes; and there shall be no more death, neither sorrow, nor crying . . . : for the former things are passed away." "God himself will be with them, and be their God." He believed in life. "For the trumpet shall sound, and the dead shall be raised incorruptible, and we shall be changed." "This corruptible must put on incorruption, and this mortal must put on immortality. . . . Then shall be brought to pass the saying that is written, Death is swallowed up in victory. O death, where is thy sting? O grave, where is thy victory?" Thank God for such a hope. And this was his hope. "O God, our help in ages past, our hope for years to come; be Thou our guide while life shall last, and our eternal home!"

CONGRESSMAN JERRY L. PETTIS: HIS STORY

Three Telegrams

House Minority Leader John J. Rhodes, before presenting the eulogy, read three telegrams addressed to Mrs. Jerry Pettis. "Just heard of the news here in Mexico of the tragic death of my longtime friend, Jerry. I was shocked speechless. My wife and I went immediately to prayer for you and the family. I always considered him to be one of my finest Christian friends in the government. He will be greatly missed." Billy Graham.

This is from George Bush, Envoy of the United States to the People's Republic of China. The Bushes for many years were neighbors of the Pettises in Washington. "Dear Shirley, Barb and I are crushed. Our hearts ache for your family and for our country too. The Congress will miss Jerry's outstanding leadership. We Bushes who love him as neighbor and friend will treasure every happy memory of this wonderful human being. When a little time is past, come be with us in Peking. We wish we were there now to hold out our hands to you. Much love, Barbara and George Bush."

This telegram: "Betty and I were shocked by the news of Jerry's tragic death, and we send our deepest sympathy to you and your family. Words have so little meaning, but we want you to know you are in our thoughts at this time. Jerry was a dear friend and a great American, as well as a devoted husband and father. We hope that the memory of his life will comfort you and that you may find consolation in knowing that Jerry's lifelong commitment to our nation will long be remembered by the people he served so well. His legacy of public service will be a tribute to his memory. We'll be praying for you and your family in the difficult days ahead." Gerald R. Ford."

Eulogy of Jerry L. Pettis
by House Minority Leader John J. Rhodes

The flag has been lowered over the White House in memory of Jerry Pettis at the orders of President Ford.

It is my sad duty, but one I fulfill with great pride, to express the deep sense of loss the entire Congress of the United States feels at this time. In a more personal sense I hope I can express for myself the depth of my own sense of loss at the death of a valued and trusted friend. I also wish to express the sympathy of my fellow Arizonans at the passing of a native son. He was a native Arizonan, and we are very proud of him. He too was proud to have been born in our state. Our brother Jerry Pettis was a man of many parts and a possessor of many talents. He was richly endowed by his Creator with a fine mind and sound body, but, more importantly, he also had

114

the gift of the great desire to become involved in the matters of importance to his fellowman. His ambitions were not for himself, but for a great role in furthering the interests of his world, his country, and all of his brothers in the fatherhood of God. His highly developed sense of values coming from deeply held religious convictions were a beacon which guided him every moment of his life.

Although he was highly successful in every walk of life he entered, he remained tolerant of others and retained his humility. His fine humor not only served to help him over many rough spots but made him a person whose companionship delighted his many friends. No profile of Jerry Pettis would be complete without mentioning his deep love for his family, his fellowmen, and particularly his constituents and his country. He also loved the House of Representatives as an institution, although he was in the forefront of many efforts to make it better and more responsive to the country's needs.

Jerry was an effective member of the great committee on Ways and Means and was the ranking minority member of the Subcommittee on Health. He was a staunch Republican, a very important member of the party; he was deputy whip of the group in the House of Representatives; he was partisan, but he was always fair. He had many friends in the Congress on both sides of the aisle. I have never heard anyone say anything bad about Jerry Pettis. I am sure that every member of the human race who knew him will say with me that the world has lost a fine man, a good man in every sense of the word. We can all be comforted by the fact that we have been privileged to know him so that we too may take pride in the accomplishments of his full and fruitful life. We may all find solace that, God willing, we shall all meet our brother Jerry in a far better place than this. May God rest his soul.

TYPICAL REACTIONS TO JERRY'S DEATH FROM OLD FRIENDS:

"The day of Jerry's funeral was a very sad one for both of us. My husband listened over a loudspeaker to the impressive program from his wheelchair in the convalescent home where he has spent the past year. Those who listened nearby were sure the service, with its music and special messages, was getting through to him, for he was sobbing as he listened.

"The following day I brought our campus paper, with a page of pictures taken at the funeral, to my husband and showed him all the pictures. When his eyes fell on the one of Jerry's flag-draped coffin carried by the pallbearers, he burst into tears. *It was as a father mourning for the loss of a son.*" —Mrs. W. I. Smith, Loma Linda, California (Dr. Smith was president of Pacific Union College for four of the five years Jerry spent there. He is now deceased.)

CONGRESSMAN JERRY L. PETTIS: HIS STORY

"What a loss to have Jerry taken from us. I did not hear the news until rather late Friday afternoon when washing dishes in our little kitchen and I turned on the radio—then let my tears fall in the dishpan. It was hard to believe, and even more so since just that morning I had been praying for him."—Mrs. A. R. Monteith, Joshua Tree, California. (Dr. Monteith had been dean of men during one or two years of Jerry's college life, and one of his teachers.)

"I had not wept for years, but when I heard of Jerry's death here in Washington, D.C.—I had chanced to turn on the radio—I could not help it. He was the brother I never had, the friend who never changed with the years." —Kenneth H. Wood, editor of the *Review and Herald*, world paper of the Seventh-day Adventist Church, and former college classmate of Jerry.

From CONGRESSIONAL RECORD—HOUSE, Feb. 27, 1975, pages H 1200 ff.

Mr. BOB WILSON. Mr. Speaker, I have taken this time to allow my colleagues to join me in paying tribute to the memory of one of the finest Members of Congress who ever stood in the well of this House, the late Jerry Pettis, who just 2 weeks ago tomorrow met with a tragic accident while on a flying trip in his own congressional district in California.

The accomplishments of Jerry Pettis on behalf of mankind, as a legislator and through numerous other endeavors, were numerous. I am sure they will be referred to many times today in the eulogies of our colleagues who grieve the tragic loss of this wonderful man. He had been an inventor, a businessman, an educator, a Christian leader, a rancher, a philanthropist, and an aviator, both in peacetime and in war; but through all of his endeavors ran a single thread of purpose—to extend a helping hand to others. His genuine friendliness toward his colleagues pierced the formality of our daily chores in the House. His untimely death is not only a great loss to Congress and our Nation, but to me personally, for he had been one of my closest friends.

As a Congressman, Jerry Pettis was a dynamic legislator, one who always contributed new ideas for solving problems, not only on a national level, but those of his constituents whom he served so well with endless energy. There was never a constituent request that did not receive his fullest effort.

As a member of the Committee on Ways and Means, he had just reached a leadership position as ranking minority member of the Subcommittee on Health when his life was cut short. His colleagues on that subcommittee, I know, are well aware of the excitement and enthusiasm Jerry Pettis had about delving into the complex question of a national health program.

APPENDIX

Jerry Pettis in one of his recent experiences had been a hospital adminis-trator and was an acknowledged expert on medical problems. During a recent visit to Red China he spent much of his time exploring Chinese medi-cal knowledge and practices, including acupuncture.

Mr. Speaker, my wife, Shirley, and I extend our deepest sympathy to his children, Yvonne, Deborah, and Peter, and especially to his widow, Shir-ley, who was always a helpmate of his political campaigning. In the conduct of his business she often attended with him the various meetings throughout his large district. She often spoke for him when he was not able to be pres-ent. She is a beautiful person in every way and we, my wife and I, extend to her our special sympathy.

Mr. STEIGER of Wisconsin. Mr. Speaker, I appreciate the gentleman from California taking this time. I must say, it does not seem possible that just 2 weeks ago tomorrow Jerry Pettis was killed in what has to be one of the saddest and most tragic plane accidents, and yet also the most ironic of accidents. From my wife, Janet, to Shirley, and [from] the Steiger family, Jerry Pettis and Shirley have been close friends. [He was] one of the men to whom I would look for guidance and counsel, one of those who came in that 90th Congress as part of the class who was elected in 1966. Jerry Pettis above and beyond anything else represented the finest ideals and qualities of a human being. He was kind to those who were his friends. He was generous to those he may never have met before, but who asked him to serve. He was incredibly good in his commitments to his fellow human beings, whether that be as a Member of this institution or as an inventor, as the gentleman from California (Mr. Bob Wilson) has said, or as a leader, at Loma Linda University as a professor in that institution, as one of the guiding lights of his church and all that he did and for his religious faith.

Jerry Pettis will long be remembered by many who have many deep feel-ings about who ought to serve in this body, and have all kinds of ideas we ought to live up to.

I must say, Mr. Speaker, the day the delegation went to Jerry's funeral will be for me and for Jan one of the saddest days we have ever experienced. It was a tribute that so many in his district came and were either in the Loma Linda University chapel or were outside that chapel. Perhaps no man could ask for more than to know that those he served had that kind of affection for one like Jerry Pettis.

He will be missed; he will be remembered. May we ever, within our own service in this body or in our own lives, strive to do half as much as he did.

Mr. BROWN of California. Mr. Speaker, I thank the gentleman from California for yielding to me. I want to commend him for taking this time to allow us to express our individual respect and regard for Jerry Pettis.

Mr. Speaker, it is nearly impossible for me to convey the sense of shock

117

and deep personal loss which struck me on Friday afternoon, February 14, when I first learned of the sudden death of Jerry Pettis. I have known Jerry since he first came to Congress in 1967, when he was assigned to the House Science and Astronautics Committee on which I also served. I developed great respect for his legislative abilities and intelligence during the next few years; and I found Congressman Pettis to be a cordial companion in the many activities in which, because of our common committee assignment, we participated together. In 1968 we both took part in an inspection trip to our scientific facilities in Antarctica, and the following year we were guests together on a Los Angeles television station, providing commentary during the historic Apollo 11 mission. . . .

Mr. Speaker, I mourn the loss of a friend, the people of California's 37th District have lost a dedicated and able Representative, and the Congress shall be the less for the tragic death of one of its most capable and hard-working Members.

I extend my sympathy and heartfelt best wishes in this difficult time to those most directly affected by this tragedy: the Congressman's gracious and popular wife, Shirley; their children; and Jerry's very knowledgeable and competent staff both here and back in California.

(Space will not permit the printing of the texts of tributes from Congressmen Don H. Clausen, Ruppe, Burgener, McEwen, Lagomarsino, Charles Wilson, Buchanan, Ichord, Moss, McClory, McMahon, Edwards, Thone, Derwinski, Nix, Anderson, Waggoner, Crane, Addabbo, Morgan, Lloyd, Sebelius, de la Garza, Cederberg, Wylie, Mrs. Burke, Bevill, Leggett, Guyer, Vigorito, Lujan, Andrews, Collins, Johnson, McDade, Frey, Cotter, Fraser, Sarasin, Ford, Horton, Reuss, Nedzi, Dent, Abdnor, Rostenhowski, Gibbons, Schneebeli, Stark, John L. Burton, Phillip Burton, Corman, Danielson, Roybal, Van Deerlin, Johnson, Ketchum, Rousselot, Rhodes, Carter, Sikes, Del Clawson, Goldwater, Mrs. Mink, Pritchard, Ginn, Miller, Erlenborn, Broomfield, J. William Stanton, Clancy, Flynt, Talcott, Broyhill, Railsback, Quillen, Coughlin, Wolff, Winn, Edwards, Brown, and McKinney.

Life Sketch of Jerry L. Pettis
by Alonzo L. Baker, Ph.D.

Today we mourn the tragic passing of the most distinguished resident the city of Loma Linda has ever known. Indeed, in the roster of distinguished men and women who have come from San Bernardino County in its 125 years of history few names, if any, shine with more luster than that of Representative in the Congress, Jerry Pettis.

Jerry Lyle Pettis was born in Phoenix, Arizona, on 18 July, 1916. His father, Dwight Pettis, died when Jerry was but 15 years of age. His mother, Clora Zimmerman Pettis, now 96, lives on in Phoenix. Owing to the infirmities of years she is unable to be here today.

Jerry was the eldest of five children, three of whom survive him. A sister, Mrs. Ramona Ireland, lives in Nelson, New Zealand; two brothers, George and Wendell Pettis of Phoenix, are here today.

In addition to an adored wife, Shirley, Jerry leaves a son, Peter, 19, and a daughter, Deborah, 16. Deborah is a student in the very excellent private preparatory school, "The Bishop's School for Girls," in La Jolla. Peter is a recent graduate of the prestigious Sierra International Academy of Aeronautics in Northern California. Of the several score graduates in his class, Peter was top man in grades and scholarship. He is now a licensed commercial pilot, and a licensed flight instructor.

Three other members of the close-knit Pettis family group are the parents of Mrs. Pettis, Dr. Harold McCumber, veteran college history professor and author, and Mrs. Dorothy McCumber, and Mrs. Pettis's aunt, Dr. Maud O'Neill. These are longtime residents of Loma Linda and active participants in community life here.

Jerry Pettis took his preparatory school education in the Thunderbird S.D.A. Academy in Phoenix; his four years of college study were done at Pacific Union College in Napa County, California, from which he was graduated with high honors and as president of his class. Jerry did graduate study in speech at the University of Southern California earning a Master of Arts degree. In the school year of 1940–41 he taught speech at Union College, Nebraska.

For a time Pettis was a Seventh-day Adventist minister pastoring churches in Arizona and Colorado. Inasmuch as his parish areas were large he flew a rented plane. On a Sabbath morning he would preach in one of his churches; Sabbath afternoon in another far away; and sometimes even on a Saturday evening he would meet with a third congregation. He soon became known and publicized as "the flying parson."

It was during those years of ministry that Jerry came in contact with Elder H. M. S. Richards, an evangelist, and the world-famous Dr. Richards of the "Voice of Prophecy" radio broadcasts heard regularly around the world. Some 25 years ago Dr. Richards was the clergyman who united Shirley McCumber and Jerry Pettis in marriage. It is that same venerable Dr. Richards who shortly will present the sermon of this afternoon.

After the Pearl Harbor debacle Pettis, since his early boyhood an ardent believer in America, yearned to do something for his country then in distress. Hence he soon became an organizer for the Civil Air Patrol, known everywhere now as C.A.P. The C.A.P. is an organization of nonmilitary fliers who respond instantly when a call comes over the air for assistance in locating a lost or downed plane. They do a tremendous job of search and rescue. For years Jerry also acted as a flight instructor for young fliers who wanted to join C.A.P. I hold in my hand a telegram from General Leslie Westberg, United States Air Force, and Commander C.A.P.:

"Dear Mrs. Pettis: The entire membership of C.A.P. has been saddened by the news of your husband's tragic death. The C.A.P. has lost one of its greatest friends and most respected leaders. His personal support and untiring efforts in our behalf will continue to be an inspiration to the 61,000 members of this national volunteer organization. Although words cannot express the depth of our concern, be assured of our prayers and heartfelt sympathy."

In the last two years of WW2, 1944 and 1945, Jerry Pettis was with the Air Transport Command flying the Pacific. After the war he became a United Airlines pilot, eventually rising to the position of Special Assistant to the President of United Airlines.

Recognizing the great talents of Jerry Pettis the Adventist medical school, now known as Loma Linda Medical School, persuaded Pettis to forgo his burgeoning career in commercial aviation to become Vice-President for Public Affairs and Development. Pettis was an influential factor in the consolidation of the hitherto bifurcated school on the Loma Linda campus; also in the planning and erection of the magnificent new 450-bed Medical Center Building; also in the improvement and enlargement of library and teaching facilities here. Pettis was most active in promoting the medical school and its several affiliates to university status. He himself solicited large funds from the alumni for these improvements and expansions. Of more recent years he and Mrs. Pettis have been most liberal benefactors of the University, their gifts running six figures and more.

In the 1950's Jerry served as an executive in the office of the Los Angeles County Medical Society whose members number more than any other county medical society in America. It was during this period of time that Pettis originated the tape-recorded Audio-Digest for the thousands of busy physicians he served. When Jerry accepted the invitation of this medical school to become one of its officials he turned his Audio-Digest business over to the C.M.A., the California Medical Association, with the one proviso that all profits made from his invention should go to assist needy medical students. To the day of his death last Friday, the C.M.A. has been enabled to help deserving medical students to an amount in excess of ten million dollars.

Not many months ago a friend asked, "Jerry, of all the things you have done in your career what gives you the most satisfaction?" Without even a moment's hesitation he replied, "The gift of the Audio-Digest to the C.M.A., and its resultant aid to hundreds of medical students who needed financial help to get through medical school: that's the thing which warms my heart the most. If I am remembered at all after I am gone that's the one thing I want to be remembered for.''

Generosity and concern for others bring their own rewards to a man's heart, soul and psyche. If perchance they also pay dividends of a material worth then the doer and the giver is doubly blessed, as for example: the production of the Audio-Digest led Pettis inexorably to the invention of the magnetic tape duplicating device, thence onward to the founding of the successful Hollywood business firm known as Magnetic Tape Duplicators whose profits have run into millions of dollars.

In the estimation of many friends of Jerry Pettis his greatest accomplishment in the eight years he has been in Congress is his success in persuading the Federal Veterans' Administration to locate a new 550-bed, $71 million Veterans' Hospital on a tract of land near and adjunctive to the Loma Linda Medical School and Medical Center. Being a veteran of WW1 myself, having been a member of the American Legion for more than half a century, and a past Post-Commander in the American Legion, I applaud Congressman Pettis for his part in locating a new veterans' facility in the heart of California's Inland Empire. I am joined in this applause by the tens of thousands of veterans in Riverside, San Diego, San Bernardino, Imperial and Orange counties. I pray a suggestion from me on this somber occasion will not be deemed inappropriate. I make bold this day, and here and now, to suggest that the new hospital in America's Bi-Centennial year 1976 be named, ''The Jerry Pettis Memorial Veterans' Hospital.''

To give a faint idea of the high esteem held for Jerry Pettis you have just heard the Minority Leader in the House of Representatives, the Honorable John Rhodes, Republican Congressman from Jerry's home state of Arizona, read you three Telex wire messages from President Gerald Ford, Evangelist Billy Graham, now on a campaign in Mexico City, Mexico, and George Bush, envoy to the People's Republic of China from Peking. I have two more to read you now, the first from the greatest diplomatist America has ever had, Secretary of State, Henry Kissinger, at the moment shuttling back and forth between Cairo, Tel Aviv, Damascus, Teheran and Riyadh in another effort to prevent another fateful Middle-East War. From the Mid-East under the date of February 15, the day after Jerry's death, Henry Kissinger wired Mrs. Pettis: ''I was shocked by the news of your husband's tragic accident. His absence will be a major loss to the Congress and will diminish us all.''

How true are Kissinger's words, ''His absence will diminish us all''!

Yesterday at the McCumber residence here in Loma Linda I spent some hours looking over the hundreds upon hundreds of telegrams, mailgrams, and letters which have poured in since last Friday noon. All are addressed to Shirley who, of course, has not yet seen even a tithe of them. I was overwhelmed by the avalanche of esteem and admiration for Jerry, and the love and sympathy for Shirley. Allow me to read just one more, this one from "The Members of the San Bernardino City Council." I was more impressed by this communication than any other, and for this reason: Someone had said that "a prophet is not without honor except in his own home town and community." In my long life I have never felt called upon to challenge that statement, but I do so now! San Bernardino is the site of the headquarters office for Congressman Pettis in all his huge 37th Congressional District. Lend your ear, please, to this from San Bernardino's City Fathers, addressed to Mrs. Pettis:

"Our hearts share your sorrows in these dark hours. There is so little we mortals can do for those left behind except hold them up in prayer so God, the Father, may see them through the valley of shadow to the sunshine of His mountain top. The world will surely long remember Congressman Pettis as a giant among men who courageously stood for right and the betterment of mankind through effective government. His concern for all peoples, rich or poor, big or small, the neighbor next door or the person across the state, was without equal. This made him dear to the hearts of the people. Yes, Congressman Pettis was a great man and losing him will be felt throughout the land. May God bless and keep you in these days." (Signed: Members of the City Council, City of San Bernardino.)

If the death of Jerry Pettis constitutes an irreparable loss to California and the nation at large, his loss is even a greater blow to Seventh-day Adventism. Jerry was the first of our faith ever to sit in America's national legislature. The relationship between the office of Congressman Pettis on the Hill and our national and international headquarters a few miles away in Takoma Park has been of invaluable aid to the officials of our General Conference. However, since last Friday our linkage with the Congress through the person of a capable and dedicated Seventh-day Adventist Congressman no longer exists.

In the opinion of many of us here today Loma Linda University also has suffered a major loss in the passing of Jerry Pettis. His guidance and wise counsel is no longer available to the trustees of the University nor to the Deans of the nine schools comprising the University. Pettis was very popular and influential with the medical college alumni.

In the galaxy of names of persons who have contributed greatly to the upbuilding and upgrading of Loma Linda University are such as Dr. Percy Magan, Dr. Newton Evans, Dr. Edward Risley, Dr. G. T. Anderson, Dr. D. J. Bieber, and Dr. Robert Cleveland, and in my category last, but by no means least, is the name of Jerry Pettis. Our University will sorely miss him in the months and years ahead.

APPENDIX

A few minutes back I told you of the one thing Jerry said he hoped to be remembered for. With your sufferance let me tell you now of a few words of mine to Jerry Pettis some ten years ago which in light of developments since then now constitute a high point in my many years of life.

The first time Jerry ran for Congress he was defeated. When I heard the news in the evening of that November election night I was very disappointed. I was about to go off to bed with a heavy heart when suddenly I found myself not heading for the bedroom, but instead to my study and to my typewriter. In a minute or so I found myself writing Jerry a letter urging him to run again two years hence. I gave him two chapters out of my life story, the year 1936 chapter and the 1938 chapter.

I told him that in 1936 I aspired to be the very first Adventist ever to be elected to the Congress. I won the Republican nomination in the primary very handily. For the November election I was amply supplied with funds from men such as ex-president Herbert Hoover, Samuel F. B. Morse, of the Del Monte Properties Corporation, and others of the 8th California Congressional District which then was made up of the five counties directly south of San Francisco City and County. I told Jerry of the very active campaign I put on for seven months and of my hopes of attaining a seat in the Federal Legislature. I also told him of my narrow defeat in November, owing to the national landslide for FDR wherein he won 46 out of the 48 states.

After that recital I told Jerry I made the mistake of my life in 1938 when I turned down the importunities of Republican leaders and offers of plenteous campaign monies if I would allow my name to be put in nomination. The defeat two years before had wounded my pride and ego so much I was afraid of the risk.

Another young chap was nominated and elected, serving 14 years in the Congress, then retiring to look after his deceased father's farm and orchards.

I besought Jerry not to repeat my mistake of 30 years before. He took my advice, was elected and reelected three times more, and undoubtedly could have served in Congress many more terms were it not for the tragedy last Friday morning in the murky weather high on a mountain above Banning.

Four weeks to the day before Jerry's passing the Pettises had invited Mrs. Baker and me down to their lovely home and ranch on the slopes of Mt. Palomar overlooking the beautiful Pauma Valley with Oceanside and the blue Pacific on their western horizon. Jerry took me via four-wheel-drive jeep through his 100-acre citrus and avocado groves. In all my 76 years of living in California I have never seen a more verdant, thriving, and productive citrus and avocado grove than on the Pettis ranch. To my surprise and amazement I discovered a phase of Jerry's multifaceted interests and abilities I had not known before. Jerry has been a very skilled, scientific horticulturist for years; so skilled, so innovative and so creative in citri-culture that every year the professors at U.C.R. (University of California at Riverside, formerly a college founded for the express purpose of developing and scientific study of the citrus industry in Southern California) bring their students down to the Pettis ranch to see the great contributions Pettis has made to the growing of oranges, lemons, grapefruit, tangerines and tangelos. In my estimation Jerry Pettis is California's modern day Luther Burbank.

As Jerry and I stood on the porch of his ranch house that Friday evening and watched the golden sun sink into the waters of the Pacific beyond Catalina, Jerry said to me, "Shirley and I have built this home and developed these orchards so we may have a place to retire to some day; a home far, far away and sequestered from the busy, high-pressure life a Congressman and his wife lead. This is to be our haven of rest after a few more years in Washington."

Because of the inexplicable tragedy of last Friday that roseate future is not to be; at least, as of now. But it will be some day, of that I am sure! Here are the words of Isaiah, one of the greatest of the Bible prophets, when he foresaw the time when a new earth is to be: In that day, said Isaiah, "they shall build houses and inhabit them; they shall plant vineyards and eat the fruit of them; they shall not build and another inhabit; they shall not plant and another eat." They will not labor in vain nor bring forth for calamity; for my people, mine elect, says Jehovah of Hosts, shall for eternity enjoy the work of their hands.

Another with prophetic prescience, Ellen White, living in the early years of our 20th century, has written: "In the earth made new the redeemed shall live the Eden life in garden and field." Our beloved Jerry will be right at home in the Edenic environment!

Life Sketch of Jerry L. Pettis
by Kenneth H. Wood, Editor, *Review and Herald*

It requires the perspective of time to provide an accurate evaluation of the life of a man, and to assign him his place in history; yet even now, surrounded as we are by the dark cloud of tragic death and sorrow, it is possible to see through that cloud to the clear realization that Jerry L. Pettis was a great and good man. He was great in his pursuit of achievement, in his enormous vision of what could be accomplished, in his capabilities and talents. He was good in his devotion to his family, to his home, to his church, and to his country. He was a man of sterling character, devoted to worthwhile causes, to furthering the welfare of all the people whom he served.

He was, by birth, a Westerner, shaped by the vast deserts and plains and towering mountains. His thinking was influenced by the adventure and rest-

lessness and broad scope of opportunity which characterizes that area. Born in Phoenix, Arizona, on July 18, 1916, he fitted well the poetic appeal:
"Bring me men to match my mountains,
Bring me men to match my plains,
Men with empires in their purpose
And new eras in their brains."

He carried within himself the vital motivation for achievement which culminated in his great contribution to his country, for he was not born to wealth and ease. Throughout his early life, his education in Seventh-day Adventist parochial schools was financed almost entirely by his own efforts and this at a time when the United States was still deep in the aftermath of the Great Depression. These school years firmed and crystallized his belief in the message of his church and caused him thereafter always to regard himself as, first of all, a Seventh-day Adventist, everywhere and in all circumstances.

His college years, at Pacific Union College, about 50 miles north of San Francisco, were years of growth and development. Classmates recall that many times he worked most of the night, slept two or three hours, then attended his classes. Ever a natural leader, he became a keen student of human nature; he came to understand the needs and hopes and desires of others. He sensed the basic loneliness of the human being. This understanding and genuine interest in others resulted in his being elected to most of the major offices on his college campus, including the presidency of his senior class in 1938. One of his classmates, a close friend for 41 years, commented recently: "There was something about Jerry, a special quality, a charisma, a singleness of purpose, a clear definition of goals which, young as we were then, we all recognized. We expected him to rise to great heights—so that, when he did, it was almost as though it had been preordained."

Always a most persuasive and effective speaker, Jerry became student assistant in the Speech Department of Pacific Union College to the late, distinguished professor, Dr. Charles E. Weniger. Their friendship was close and enduring, terminated only by the death of the latter.

After college graduation, Jerry's love for the broad deserts of Arizona brought him back there as a ministerial intern. Tirelessly he criss-crossed his assigned territory, bringing God's message eloquently to all who would listen.

His penchant for overwork at one time caused his conference president to order him to take a month off, free from all platform activity. Immediately thereafter he resumed his evangelistic work.

His eloquence and superior talents soon attracted the attention of the leaders of the Seventh-day Adventist Church. He was asked to conduct evangelistic meetings in Kansas City, Missouri, where he was ordained to

CONGRESSMAN JERRY L. PETTIS: HIS STORY

the gospel ministry. In an era when youth was not looked upon favorably for leadership posts, Jerry's achievement was all the more remarkable.

It is said that one characteristic of a truly superior person is his broad spectrum of interests. By this standard, Jerry Pettis was truly superior. Time after time he entered a new and completely different professional field, stayed in it as long as was necessary to make a brilliant success, then fastened his eyes and energies on a new goal.

His speaking skills so impressed the administration of Union College, in Lincoln, Nebraska, that he was invited to join the faculty as a member of the Speech Department. This new challenge drew him inexorably, but he did not depend entirely on his intrinsic capabilities; he recognized that the world of academia had its own standards, so he put himself under a heavy study schedule at the University of Nebraska and earned his Master's Degree. Later he took further advanced work at the University of Southern California.

In addition to his professional interests during his early years, Jerry had become convinced that aviation, then somewhat in its infancy, would eventually become the most important means of transportation in the world, as well as one of the military and economic factors which would decide national superiority. During his college years, he had been fascinated by a small open cockpit plane which a friend owned. He flew as a passenger in this craft at every opportunity. Later, in Arizona, he took flying lessons and obtained his first license, to the amazement of his less visionary friends and colleagues. True to form, he continued his lessons and skills until he secured his commercial pilot's license. At the time of his death, he was the only member of the House of Representatives to hold such a license.

It was almost as though he had foreseen World War II and had known that flight instructors would be vital to the war effort of the United States, for he filled this role as well as that of an Air Transport Command Pilot in the Pacific theater during the war years. College classmates in far-flung corners of the earth in various types of service for church and country sometimes looked up and there was Jerry, having just brought in a transport plane to Guam, or Fiji, or New Guinea. On one flight to Shanghai, China, he made it a point to visit the Shanghai Sanitarium, operated by the Seventh-day Adventist Church, which he had heard so much about from close friends who had grown up as missionaries' children there.

His marriage to the former Shirley McCumber, marked the beginning of one of the most brilliantly successful husband and wife teams on the American scene. Shirley fully understood when she married him that her life would be one of intensity, of pressure, and of conquering "the hill beyond the hill beyond the hill." Her complete devotion and supportive attitude sustained Jerry through the remainder of his life, a life which took on ever larger dimensions.

From 1948–1960 he was a special assistant to the president of United Airlines. Then a new horizon beckoned, and he entered the world of business. Applying his tireless energy and ambition in this field, he founded the Magnetic Tape Duplicators—the world's largest user and duplicator of magnetic tape. He also established the Audio-Digest Foundation, a non-profit organization furnishing monthly education tapes to physicians to keep them abreast of new developments in their field. Foundation earnings are held in a trust fund and are used to provide scholarships for needy medical students throughout the United States.

During this period he accepted the post of Executive Secretary of the California Medical Association. His expertise in the field of medicine and health care served him later in good stead in his political life.

While devoting his efforts to the business world, he continued his interest in education, and from 1948–1964 served as a professor of Economics at Loma Linda University in Southeastern California. From 1960–1964 he was the Vice-President of this institution in charge of development, and from 1960–1967 he was Chairman of the Board of Counselors. He played a key role in funding and building the $25 million Loma Linda University Medical Center. The new $71 million, 550-bed Veterans' Hospital in Loma Linda is also being built as a direct result of his efforts both in and out of the Congress.

With so many worlds conquered, he looked about him much as Tennyson's "Ulysses" did:

> "I am a part of all that I have met;
> Yet all experience is an arch wherethro'
> Gleams that untravell'd world whose margin fades
> Forever and forever when I move.
> How dull it is to pause, to make an end,
> To rust unburnish'd, not to shine in use!
> As though to breathe were life!
> Life piled on life were all too little . . ."

The world of the political arena now engaged his interest and ambition. Nurtured in an age when patriotism and service to one's country were considered cardinal virtues, he had always been an interested spectator of the political scene. Now having made his decision to run for the House of Representatives from California's 33rd district, he was elected to the 90th Congress on November 8, 1966. Subsequently, he was reelected to the 91st, the 92nd, the 93rd, and, last November, the 94th Congress. [Through a redistribution of territory the 33rd district became the 37th.]

He was a member of the powerful Ways and Means Committee, which writes the laws on all personal and corporate taxes, Social Security and related health care programs, trade and tariff regulations and other vital areas. Since joining the Committee, Congressman Pettis had helped to author comprehensive welfare reforms, Social Security increases totaling 15 percent, middle-income oriented tax reforms, to airport and airways funding regulations, new trade agreements and a revenue-sharing plan designed to help states and localities.

In the 94th Congress, he had been appointed Chief Minority Deputy Whip. As the third most senior Republican on the Ways and Means Committee, he was the Ranking Republican on the Subcommittee on Health; he also served on the Trade and Oversight Subcommittees.

Congressman Pettis also served on the special Congressional Task Force on National Health, and was a member of the Earth Resources and Population Task Force. He was an advisor to the National Commission on Fire Prevention and Control and was a member of the Republican Congressional Policy Committee.

As an acknowledged expert in the health care field, the Congressman was in great demand as a speaker advocating new approaches to improve national health care delivery systems. His interest and background led to his recognized role as a strong advocate of improved educational programs.

The *Christian Science Monitor* honored him in its choice of Outstanding Congressmen and he won the Watchdog of the Treasury Award for support of thrift in government spending, a 100 percent National Security Index rating put out by the American Security Council, and numerous commendations for service and leadership in Congress.

And so the curtain has fallen on a life filled with dedication and achievement. Was there one place, one spot which for him meant rest and tranquillity, easement from incessant work? There was such a place—his ranch among his citrus and avocado groves in Southeastern California. There he and Shirley cherished precious peace and privacy. There he spent treasured hours with his children, Peter and Debbie, to whom he leaves the precious legacy of his desire for excellence.

At the time of his death, he was a member of the Loma Linda University Seventh-day Adventist Church. But when he was in Washington, D.C., he regularly attended the Capital Memorial Church off Connecticut Avenue, the Sligo Church, the Takoma Park Church, or other suburban churches. He was a familiar sight to other worshipers, his Bible always with him.

Jerry L. Pettis, a man for all seasons, a man to match mountains, died on February 14, 1975, at the age of 58. He awaits the call of his Saviour, in whom he believed and whom he served.

He leaves his beloved wife, Shirley; three children, Yvonne, Peter, and Debbie, and hosts of devoted friends from all parts of the world and all walks of life.

The world is better for his having lived.